Non-Punitive
School Discipline

Non-Punitive School Discipline

Relational Practices to Help Students Overcome Problem Behaviors

Adam H. Frank

Foreword by Harry Wong

TEACHERS COLLEGE PRESS

TEACHERS COLLEGE | COLUMBIA UNIVERSITY
NEW YORK AND LONDON

Published by Teachers College Press,® 1234 Amsterdam Avenue, New York, NY 10027

Copyright © 2022 by Teachers College, Columbia University

Front cover illustration and design by Peter Donahue.

Library of Congress Cataloging-in-Publication Data is available at loc.gov

ISBN 978-0-8077-6726-9 (paper)
ISBN 978-0-8077-6727-6 (hardcover)
ISBN 978-0-8077-8118-0 (ebook)

Printed on acid-free paper
Manufactured in the United States of America

I've written this book to help educators—both teachers and principals—win with students, especially misbehaving students. My aim is to encourage educators by helping them to grow and acquire skills and strategies and new ways of thinking so that they may no longer experience frustration or discouragement when dealing with student misbehavior. My hope is that educators will go on to experience the joy and satisfaction that can come not only from working with certain students, but from winning with such students so that behaviors change and students grow in positive ways through making good choices!

Contents

Foreword

"What do I do to the kid who . . ." is the question I get often. My answer is the same as what Adam Frank says in his book, *Non-Punitive School Discipline: Relational Practices to Help Students Overcome Problem Behaviors*. You do not do anything *to* someone. It's what you do *with* someone, and that is the thesis of this book. All educators can learn how to win with misbehaving students! The emphasis is on *with*.

Most behavior problems in the classroom are caused. For instance, there are no assigned seats, no place to put the backpack, no indication of where to put a name on an assignment, no schedule or agenda, and no signal as to how to come to attention. So, the students come to class and wander around until the teacher yells—yes, yells—at the class to sit down and come to attention. In these situations, it is not the student's fault if misbehavior surfaces.

Dr. Frank acknowledges that it is imperative that you have an organized classroom and a skillful approach when working with misbehaving students. For that, I am most pleased that he cited my work on classroom management in *THE First Days of School*. He writes, "Having clear expectations matters! Defining simple, yet meaningful procedures is paramount for helping students know how to behave in an educational, peer-based environment" (p. 11, this volume).

When the school year begins, I ask my students why they go to certain stores and restaurants. The answer always comes to "they are organized." I tell them that this class is organized, and it is so that you will all succeed; I am here to help you succeed.

Just as you like businesses that are consistent, the most important condition to establish in a classroom is *consistency*. Consistency refers to a classroom environment that is predictable and stable. There is no yelling or screaming at students because they know how the classroom functions and is organized. Students (and teachers) want a safe, happy, and consistent classroom. If the student does not do something correctly, I simply say, with a firm smile, "And what's the procedure, please?"

Students crave structure. Students do not welcome surprises or embrace disorganization and inconsistency. They want a plan. It is extremely important to realize that many students come from disorganized, unstructured home environments where chaos abounds. As Dr. Frank says, "Their home lives are chaotic, their emotions are confusing, their situations are frustrating, and on top of all this, they lack wisdom and experience" (p. 145, this volume). Give them a well-managed, organized classroom with clear, daily practices and procedures, and they will respond positively.

Students succeed in a classroom when they know what is happening. Students do not like to be in classrooms where they do not know what is going to happen next. Students like consistency as it creates a school climate where everyone knows what to expect and what to do and can work in an environment that is safe and inviting.

Dr. Frank's book is based on his experience as a practitioner. He shows how he shifts the emphasis from discipline as a stand-alone product to discipline within the skillful practice of a purposeful relationship.

The book provides a multitude of strategies and resources that can help educators and principals when working with students in discipline situations. I agree with him when he states, "Effective discipline practices that are relationally based and skillfully applied certainly can make a huge difference, changing the behaviors of many misbehaving students" (p. 57).

Dr. Frank articulately explains, "Discipline, when done correctly, is a loving process. It is meant to correct and teach. It is meant to guide a ship in the right direction" (p. 7). Thus, effective teachers develop a relational experience with a misbehaving student.

—Harry Wong,
author of THE First Days of School,
THE Classroom Management Book,
and THE Classroom Instruction Book

Acknowledgments

My wife, Katie, has been a continual source of encouragement over the course of my career in education. She has always believed in me. She's always supported my efforts and advocated for my leadership.

I also want to thank my children, Tyler and Emmy. They are deeply loved and are uniquely special in so many ways! I hope they too develop a continual love for learning and growth and pursue a life that seeks to positively influence others.

Additionally, I'd like to acknowledge my former dissertation chair, Dr. Tom Poetter at Miami University. After I completed the original manuscript for this book, he told me, "Reach out to the best publishers. Like many people, you may not receive interest in your book, but you won't know until you try! Go for it!" Similar to the quote, "You miss all the shots you don't take," I followed his advice, and I received immediate interest from multiple publishers. Thank you Dr. Poetter for helping me to become a better writer in my PhD program, and thank you for the timely advice to go big with this book!

Introduction

A growing attitude in education is that student discipline is somehow inappropriate. Generally speaking, if you work in a school with a typical student population, then you *know* you can't get rid of student discipline. It would be like raising a child without disciplining them. Or running a city without laws. It would mean believing that students don't need boundaries, correction, and healthy accountability.

However, many times student discipline is grossly mishandled, inequitable, and unjust. Rarely does a student demonstrate healthy change because of rigid approaches to discipline. Consistency is essential; however, as will be discussed in this book, discipline needs to be implemented within the broader context of a *relationship* that is guided by a skilled adult.

This book seeks to merge two positions: one that values the role of discipline (when it is warranted) and the other that prioritizes relationships and giving the student a path toward growth. Discipline and relationships don't need to be mutually exclusive concepts! This is why I refer to my approach as *relational discipline*. Some educators emphasize the role of discipline so much that it appears punitive. They might not recognize this perception, but when dissected, their approach is often more concerned with *what discipline the student gets* instead of *how the student can change.* Conversely, there are educators on the opposite side of the spectrum who value relationship-building to the point of neglecting student accountability. In doing so, the misbehaving student learns that his actions don't have consequences.

The intent of this book is to share the strategies and resources that I have developed throughout my career—strategies and resources that have worked for me as I've worked with students for almost 2 decades. It is a book based on one person's experience as a practitioner, building on the theoretical foundation for the development of that practice. This book promotes the practice of school discipline, but within an approach that is relational and strategic. Much of this book seeks to *shift* the emphasis from discipline as a stand-alone product to discipline within the *skillful* practice of a purposeful relationship. My aim is to help educators think about discipline *differently*, and to help educators to shift how they position themselves with their students, becoming savvier in how they administer discipline while maintaining a positive relationship with their students.

In schools, we need to make a shift away from focusing on punishment to *fostering accountability*. Both involve consequences, but the latter is more likely to preserve the relationship, creating a platform for future growth. When discipline must exist, it needs to be relational. Educators can succeed with misbehaving students if they multiply their "tricks of the trade" and adopt a discipline philosophy that is more about accountability and less about punishment.

In this book, I explain the practice of relational discipline. I have found the relational stance, strategies, and resources in these chapters to be very useful, both for myself and for teachers and schools with whom I have shared them, fostering many more success stories with students than unfortunate failures. The strategies and resources that I share are meant to be used by teachers, school administrators, and schools. They can be used by individual teachers, leaders, and coaches and for professional development and in professional learning communities. Additionally, it can be used in teacher and principal preparation programs.

As educators, it is important to keep in mind that *the behavior is not the student*. Rather, the student is a child who momentarily or frequently exhibits certain behaviors, whether or not they are desirable. Every individual makes mistakes—even adults. The goal is not punishment, but meaningful correction. Through a mistake, educators can help students grow and become better.

*   *   *

In Chapter 1, readers will find an explanation of how the concept of non-punitive, relational discipline originated in my own career and became a hallmark practice in my work with students. Also, readers will learn about the theoretical framework and important authors that have shaped the approach described in this book. Educators will find that there is available to them a "balanced and realistic approach" to non-punitive school discipline.

In Chapter 2, I will explain the practice of relational discipline. The first part focuses on the way the adult *positions* themself in the relationship with the student. This positionality is practical, yet it is also a mental shift from what might be traditional thinking. It is nuanced but powerful in how it can transform the relationship between the adult and the student. Included in this chapter are tips for preventing students from perceiving a "versus" stance. Taken together these tips constitute a highly effective approach to keeping a discipline conversation productive rather than destructive. The second part of relational discipline pertains to the *words* the educator chooses to use. Words have enormous effects on relationships, emotions, and perceptions. What we say and how we say it can drastically impact the trajectory of a relational situation.

Chapter 3 discusses some misconceptions about school discipline. I think that practitioners will appreciate the alternative ideas that are shared within this chapter.

In Chapter 4, you will read about several strategies that I have found to be successful when working with students. Throughout my career, I've not only used these strategies but shared them with other teachers and principals.

Chapter 5 includes multiple resources and conceptual models that I have created and used in schools where I have worked. They are practical, and they allow educators to address specific situations in effective ways. I've seen multiple schools benefit from adopting and implementing these resources. Feel free to adapt them to fit your unique school and relevant circumstances.

Chapter 6, the final chapter of this book, contains scenarios for readers to try out relationship-based approaches with students displaying common forms of misbehavior. These scenarios can be used by educators to foster professional discussions about how to respond to a variety of discipline situations. The scenarios depict challenging behaviors that educators must learn to face. Students will at times misbehave! Therefore, how can we learn to *win* with misbehaving students in a relational and effective way? Again, please allow me to be clear: *Winning* applies to both teachers and students. The scenarios allow educators to work through common experiences that *seem* to magnify a challenging student behavior, which then encourages educators to rethink how they would *relate* to the student without excusing certain behaviors.

All educators can learn how to win with misbehaving students—emphasis on *with*. Discipline *and* relationships can coexist! Every parent knows this to be true. I love helping other people find success. It is why I love teaching, coaching, and leadership. By sharing what has worked for me, I've been able to help educators and school administrators in their work with challenging students. My hope is that the information in this book will also lead readers to experience the satisfaction of engaging relational discipline to address behaviors while respecting students and showing them a path toward personal growth.

CHAPTER 1

A Balanced and Realistic Approach

While studying to become a teacher, I had a professor who relentlessly ranted about the importance of classroom management. In many ways, his curriculum focused less on instructional theory and more on how to prevent, redirect, and if necessary, discipline student misbehavior. He would often say, "If you can't manage your own classroom, there's no way you can provide good instruction." He believed that the first order of business in teaching is classroom management. Once good classroom management is in place, then sound instructional practice can result.

It wasn't until after I had become a teacher, while working with student teachers, that I realized the absence of classroom management curricula in most teacher education programs at the undergraduate and graduate levels. Why is this still the case? What good is instructional theory or sound teaching practices if the students aren't made, or better yet motivated, to behave? Absent an orderly classroom, how can students be positioned to learn?

I can remember working with a veteran teacher during my first three years in teaching. We worked together on the same "team" at a middle school. For sake of confidentiality, we'll call her Jenny. She had a fun, vibrant personality. She was very caring and had great rapport with her middle school students. Among the teachers on our team, she had some of the best ideas for interactive, project-based lessons— lessons that were based on inquiry-learning and allowed student choice and ownership. However, I always felt sorry for her because she ended most days feeling defeated by her students' misbehavior. Despite her great personality, kid-friendly demeanor, and brilliant lessons, she didn't know classroom management. Consequently, teaching had become frustrating. The students were regularly "bouncing off the walls" in her classroom. I knew this for many reasons. For one, she would regularly admit how "awful" her students were in terms of their behavior. Second, on many occasions I had walked in her room and witnessed for myself the self-admitted chaos. Third, the other teachers on our team and I taught the *same* students and they never acted that way in any of our classes. Students would even say to me and other teachers, "Yeah, we are horrible for her." Her dilemma has stuck with me. How unfortunate it was that someone like her, who was skilled at teaching and truly cared about being a teacher, hated teaching and being a teacher because she didn't know how to manage student behaviors in the classroom?

As I progressed through my career, later as a high school teacher and coach, I found there to be many more teachers like Jenny. I also began to realize that there were so many other teachers who *never* had problems with student behavior. And of course, there are the many teachers somewhere in the middle who find success managing student behaviors in their classrooms on most days, but occasionally have a bad day or find it impossible to deal with a particular student. In education, teachers sometimes can be heard to say, "It must be a full moon" or "It's almost Friday!" often as a direct result of their frustration with current student misbehavior. Rather than look down on teachers who battle the "daily war"—as it can sometimes be called—with students, my endeavor is to support them in the trenches so they can begin to *win* with misbehaving students. With the adoption of a different mindset and some strategic changes to their classroom management, the daily exhaustion of dealing with misbehaving students can end once and for all!

As I moved into the role of assistant principal, and practiced building-level student discipline at four different school districts, I have taken time to reflect on classroom management in an effort to put together a practical approach that can be put into words, packaged in an understandable framework, and then shared with other educators. Much of what is included in this approach is based on my own experience and practices, whether learned from the talented professor at my undergraduate university, the experience I gained when working for a short time at a juvenile detention facility, the sharpening of my own classroom management skills as a middle and high school teacher, or the decade-long work I've spent with student discipline as an assistant principal and school principal. Along the way, I've been heavily influenced by Harry and Rosemary Wong's (2001) book, *The First Days of School.* My practice has also been informed by the classic work of John Dewey (1938), the insights of Peter Senge et al. (2012), the penetrating perspective of the much beloved and admired Fred Rogers (2019), and the analysis of how outstanding teachers succeed by Martin Haberman

(1995). The work of A. Wade Boykin and Pedro Noguera (2011) serves as a reminder of current and past inequitable discipline practices that have favored White students over student of color, and that we must strive in our work to eradicate inequitable practices. Relational discipline is structured to accomplish this.

Student discipline is, suffice to say, not my life's passion! However, it is a component of working with youth that cannot be entirely separated from quality instruction and sound pedagogy. Young people will make mistakes. They will, at times, need to be disciplined. Discipline, when done correctly, is a loving process. It is meant to correct and teach. It is meant to guide a ship in the right direction. What loving parent doesn't discipline their own children?

I did my student teaching at an urban high school, where I saw several of my students exit to a juvenile detention facility. While there, I decided to work for a season at that juvenile detention facility, learning more about how to deal with challenging youth than at any other point in my career. Afterwards, I taught 3 years at an affluent middle school and then 5 more years at the high school in the same school district. During that time, I also learned an array of invaluable lessons from being a varsity head coach. For example, I learned that clear communication yields far better results than yelling or coercion.

Next, I worked as part-teacher, part-administrator at that high school, learning the ropes of school discipline at the office level. Then, I worked another decade as a full-time assistant principal, primarily responsible for working with students through school discipline. I have never enjoyed getting students in trouble. However, by working with students through school discipline, I have been able to help students learn some of life's most important lessons. Many times, suspensions still resulted, but the conversations that preceded and followed the discipline were for some, life-changing. My PhD in educational leadership concentrated on employee–management relations, organizational leadership, and change theory, but much of my practice up to this point in my career has been in school discipline. Even after becoming a high school principal, I continually find myself sharing my experiences, strategies, and resources on school discipline with my administrative team and other educators within my school and district.

I decided to write this book for several reasons. My first reason is rooted in an *encouraging* experience. I began presenting the essence of my approach at an annual workshop at a local university. The presentation was for veteran educators who voluntarily signed up for my session to obtain continual learning credits for their professional licenses or employment. I entitled the presentation, "Relational Discipline." Every year, after each presentation, I would read through the comments made by various participants in their postpresentation reflections. Each time, I was amazed at how new and different the veteran teachers found the presentation to be. To me, it was simple. To me, I was just sharing how I approached student discipline.

I began to realize that many teachers, even really good teachers, needed and even craved help with managing student behaviors. I've seen educators benefit from hearing about and putting into practice many of the ideas that are now contained in this book. Recognizing this impact, I now want to share these strategies and resources with a broader base of educators to assist their navigation of effective student discipline. Below are some of the comments made by educators who attended my workshop on relational discipline:

- ". . . one of the most 'effective' and 'useful' presentations I've seen in many years!!! A+++!!!"
- "Wow! Want more . . . !!!"
- "[This] approach to relational discipline is a *new approach* to something educators have been dealing with since education began."
- "Dr. Frank's approach to discipline is the first of its kind that I have seen used practically in a school."
- "[The] presentation demonstrated that it is possible to maintain fidelity to rigor and discipline without being rigid or hemmed in by the rules."
- "I gained a lot of great ideas and strategies to take back to my classroom during this session."
- "[The presentation] offered some very easy approaches to discipline that I can take back and apply now."
- "I thought [this presentation] on relational discipline was one of the best sessions I've ever been to in 22 years as an educator."

In this book, I explain relational discipline while providing the "more" that educators want. Similar to some of the above comments, I trust that you will find the strategies and resources in this book to be "practical," so you can go back and "apply now" what is being shared.

My second reason for writing this book is rooted in a *discouraging* experience. I was reading through a recently published book on school discipline and restorative practices. Halfway through the book, I set it down and said to myself:

> It is finally time for me to write a book about "relational discipline"! There is *nothing* in this book [the book I was reading], and really so many other books, that say anything truly meaningful and practical for educators on the topic of school discipline. The concepts are great, but so much is vague. So much are general niceties. Most try to portray a mythical world where discipline isn't needed. I feel like other educators read these things and say, as I do, "Okay, yeah! I'd like to see that idea work with my students!" or "Are you kidding me, that would never work—it sounds good, but it isn't realistic."

Please don't misunderstand me. The book I read wasn't horrible. However, it didn't provide concrete, practical methods. It discussed great concepts but lacked the "nuts and bolts." It lacked what I believe educators are eager to know: "*When* a student does something or says something that requires accountability and appropriate discipline, *how* do I handle the student–adult relationship in a meaningful way that fosters authentic learning?"

The third motivation for writing this book came from realizing that there aren't many books written on school discipline, particularly in re-gard to how to effectively *win* with misbehaving students. Perhaps this is one reason why my annual presentation on relational discipline was so novel and favorably embraced by educators. There are many books and much research written about the *problems* with school discipline, but very few written that offer the *solutions* for how to practice school discipline more effectively. If you search for a book on school or student discipline on the Internet, you will be hard pressed to find one that provides good old-fashioned strategies and resources that are practical and actually work. Again, there are great books on the topic at-large, but not many that provide specific approaches to real-world situations when working with misbehaving students. There are some great books and educational methods that talk about how to *prevent* behaviors that lead to discipline, but how should educators *interact* with students and *manage* behavior *when* discipline is required? As a result, I've written this book to help fill this void. This book provides balanced, realistic approaches for successfully dealing with student misbehavior. Every educator can learn how to *win* with misbehaving students!

Again, please don't misunderstand me. I completely agree with doing everything possible to, ideally, avoid student discipline. I whole-heartedly support restorative practices and social–emotional learning. Actually, I believe the contents of this book are perfectly aligned with those practices. However, the reality that many books fail to address is how to handle the student–adult relationship when discipline is undeniably warranted. When all of the preventative practices meant to curtail student misbehavior fail, then what? This book provides solutions for this reality. Much of the writing and presentations on restorative practices discuss how to shift discipline from punishment to authentic learning and new opportunities for growth—which I completely agree with—but fail to explain *how* educators can *implement* discipline in a relational, and yes, restorative way. What comes *before* restoration? Unfortunately, in many cases, discipline! Therefore, how can educators issue disciplinary measures in a way that *wins* with the misbehaving student, so that restorative practices are more likely to succeed in the aftermath? Many of the answers, I hope, you will find in this book.

The topic of school discipline can be controversial. I know from experience how difficult it can be to explain and discuss the topic in front of a large group of educators. It is hard because many social dynamics exist in a group setting. Some people are listening with full attention. Other people are listening halfway. Many people have other things on their minds. People interpret a presenter's words in different ways. Assumptions are often made, and there usually aren't opportunities to ask questions or clarify information. With the topic of school discipline, some people default to thinking, "This approach is too 'soft'—it condones misbehavior." Others think, "This approach is too strict—if you truly care about the students, you wouldn't discipline them."

Furthermore, most presentations are rather brief, which discourages necessary explanation, clarification, and specific qualifications of complex concepts. However, if the presentation is too long, you will lose people's attention. Some people are living with bad experiences from previous student situations, feeling resentful about how a certain discipline scenario was handled. One person in the crowd might make a comment or ask a question that derails the intent of the presentation. Confusion and unintended messages can result. Nonetheless, discussion about school discipline needs to happen. Senge et al. (2012) declare, "We live in a world of self-generating beliefs that remain largely untested," (p. 101) and that "unexamined mental models limit people's ability to change" (p. 100).

As an antidote, a book study can provide a wonderful learning experience for a large group. One of the great things about reading is that it occurs in private, operating along the reader's own timeline. Furthermore, information is processed differently by each reader. Each reader is given the necessary time to "chew on" a new idea. As cognitive dissonance naturally occurs in a person's mind, he can wrestle with this imbalance in a nonthreatening environment and manner. Then, readers can come together to discuss what they've read along with any thoughts, questions, and/or implications. I recommend using this book to foster healthy and thoughtful professional development. Schools might focus on parts of the book or all of it. This book is meant to be a resource—a handbook—to help educators *win* with misbehaving students.

Furthermore, this book can be a useful resource to share with educators who are struggling with classroom management or who are experiencing frustration with misbehaving students. This book can be a practical resource for principals and administrative teams. Certainly, this book can be used in university classrooms as institutions prepare future teachers for the realities they will likely face in the classroom, helping them to be ready to win with misbehaving students *before* they are thick in the trenches. Likewise, this book can assist universities in preparing future school administrators and coordinators.

As I've mentioned, the contents of this book are based on almost 2 decades of my personal experience working with students in public education. However, the practical and interpersonal approach of nonpunitive school discipline owes a debt to both Harry and Rosemary Wong's (2001) book, *The First Days of School,* and Dale Carnegie's (1936) timeless piece, *How to Win Friends and Influence People.* The book is also situated within the theoretical context of A. Wade Boykin and Pedro Noguera's (2011) work, *Creating the Opportunity to Learn: Moving from Research to Practice to Close the Achievement Gap.*

Having clear expectations matters! Defining simple, yet meaningful procedures is paramount for helping students know how to behave in an educational, peer-based environment. Harry and Rosemary Wong believe clear expectations matter. They believe all good teaching flows from a well-designed and orderly classroom. They suggest that teachers close their eyes and say to themselves, "This is what I want to accomplish. Now, if the students will only do these three things . . ." (2001, p. 149). The Wongs promote "discipline with a plan" (p. 141). Being well prepared is half the battle!

Carnegie's (1936) *How to Win Friends and Influence People* has also shaped my theoretical framework when working with students. His work is often referred to as one of the greatest books on interpersonal relationships. It was written many decades before the popularity of self-help literature, promoting the use of emotional intelligence in interpersonal communication. The essential assumption of Carnegie's book is that it is far easier to learn to win with people than to battle with them. However, doing so requires both humility *and* skill. Much of his book seeks to convince readers that people are persuaded more by affective tactics than by coercive means.

Furthermore, there must be an awareness of diversity when working with students. Many of our schools look different from one another and every school consists of a diverse population. Boykin and Noguera (2011) assert, "Despite the confusion that surrounds the ways Americans think about it, race continues to have a profound effect upon life experiences in our society" (p. 18). They cite the work of Irvine (1990) and Ware (2006) in advocating a teaching approach known as "warm-demander pedagogy," which "may be particularly effective with Black students" (p. 76). Boykin and Noguera explain:

> This method entails sternness (to the point of reprimanding students who don't live up to expectations) in a way that conveys compassion, unyielding support, and nurturance. (p. 76)

That method is consistent with the approach in my book for all students but must be extended with conscious regard for the fact that students enter the classroom with varied cultural and societal experiences.

Another brilliant text that has shaped my thinking is Martin Haberman's (1995) *Star Teachers of Children in Poverty.* The description on the back cover of his book states, "Dr. Haberman shares composites from more than 1,000 interviews . . . to illustrate how star teachers think and behave differently from those who fail with students or quit the profession." In the book, Haberman states:

> [Star teachers] do not believe that punishment can, in any real sense, be educative. They use them only as a last resort, and recognize that punishments indicate a failure on their part, or that they may have given up on a youngster. (p. 9)

This statement is difficult to accept by any educator who *desires* punitive measures when working with students. However, in discussing punishment, Haberman is implicitly acknowledging that students will at times misbehave. Instead of focusing on punishment, Haberman believes it is incumbent upon the adult to handle discipline situations in educative ways. That is what "star teachers" do!

Let's take a moment to discuss the word "educative," since Haberman brings our attention to it. We often hear that things are educational or education-based. Seldom do we use the word "educative." This word was popularized by John Dewey, one of the greatest thinkers in philosophy, particularly in the field of education. In *Experience and Education*, Dewey (1938) explains "certain conditions which must be fulfilled" (p. 90) "to discriminate between experiences that are worth while educationally and those that are not" (p. 33). Dewey explains:

> The belief that all genuine education comes through experience does not mean that all experiences are genuinely or equally *educative* [emphasis added] . . . Any experience is mis-educative that has the effect of arresting or distorting the growth of further experience. (p. 25)

Applying Dewey's thinking to the topic of student behavior and discipline, punishment, as it is traditionally understood, is almost always "mis-educative." This aligns with Haberman's assertion that punishment indicates failure on the part of the adult. Any experience or a compilation of noneducative experiences could be "mis-educative" if it "has the effect of arresting or distorting the growth of further experiences" (Dewey, 1938, p. 25). How often does school discipline fail to yield future growth? However, when done differently, school discipline can become educative. I've experienced it in my own interactions with students. As educators, we want all student situations to be educative. That is, we want every student experience to result in authentic learning. Using the approach of non-punitive school discipline is meant to be educative. That is the intent.

In *Experience and Education*, Dewey (1938) also writes about "situations." He defines a situation as "any normal experience" when the emotions and intellect of a person "interacts" with an outside object or environment (pp. 42–44). The concept of a situation is a fundamental condition of an educative experience. Dewey stresses:

> The statement that individuals live in a world means, in the concrete, that they live in a series of situations. (p. 43)

He continues:

> [A]ttentive care must be devoted to the conditions which give each present experience a worthwhile meaning. (p. 49)

For example, a boy reading a book is a situation—assuming the boy is in fact reading. If he is daydreaming instead, then the situation is between him and the images he conjures in his mind. Two students interacting in a discussion or debate is a situation. A school administrator sitting in the back of a classroom, observing a lesson is a situation. A student listening to a teacher explain content in preparation for a test is a situation. A student misbehaving is a situation. Administering school discipline is a situation. The quality of these situations defines the quality of our experience in education.

Dewey (1938) expounds upon this concept by discussing "social situations." The most meaningful situations, that are most educative, are often social in nature. He claims, "all human experience is ultimately social" (p. 38). Therefore, if student situations involving discipline are merely transactional, that is, a matter of punishing X behavior with Y consequence, then one might question whether that scenario was actually a social situation according to Dewey's definition. If not, then it is merely artificial. Non-punitive school discipline is based on social interaction—on social situations. Therefore, effective school discipline should be educative—it should foster relational experiences and interactions that lead to authentic learning, which hopefully leads to changed behavior.

There are many other important thinkers and pieces of literature that align with the theoretical lens that serves as the foundation for this book. These include renowned restorative justice experts Howard Zehr (2002) and Kay Pranis (2005). Also consistent with the ideas in this book is recent work by Margaret Searle (2013) and Ruby Payne (2018), which promote social–emotional interactions with students. However, Wong and Wong's (2001) framework for clear, yet meaningful boundaries combined with the social–emotional intelligence latent in the work of Carnegie (1936) and Dewey (1938), and the student-first mentality of Haberman (1995), serve as the main influences for my concept and approach of non-punitive school discipline.

I've thoroughly enjoyed working with students throughout my career. With each new job, the context and dynamics of my role with students have changed. As a middle school teacher, I was able to teach the same students for 3 consecutive years, helping them develop through the enormously formative years of early adolescence. As a high school teacher, I was able to sharpen my craft as an instructional mentor as I watched students develop a love for Social Studies and learning in general. It was so enjoyable to watch students succeed, moving with increasing confidence from point A to point B. As a varsity coach, I loved the thrill of "game time." It was so much fun to experience winning as a group and to learn together through a loss. During the past decade, I have worked as a school principal dealing primarily with student discipline and student issues. Although this work often leads to a short tenure because you're always dealing with "bad" things and "getting kids in trouble," potentially creating a wearisome work environment, I, to be honest, have found it to be incredibly rewarding. As I've stated in this book, working with students through discipline situations can create endless opportunities to unfold new perspectives and authentic growth in students. It allows for one-on-one conversations that can solicit raw emotions, confessed thoughts, and life-changing learning. When treated through this kind of lens, it is an awesome endeavor!

However, when working with students through discipline, the concept of justice is always front and center. Typically, someone or something has been wronged. Either a teacher has been disrespected, another student has been hurt or mistreated, property has been damaged, or a classroom has been disrupted. When dealing with the misbehaving student, you must remember the concept of justice. In other words, accountability needs to occur. Boundaries need to be upheld. Truths and expectations need to be reinforced. Likewise, remedy and restoration should exist. All of this can be done in love and with gentleness.

A significant warning and noble responsibility must be given when working with students through discipline: Never, absolutely never, should a student receive unjust or unwarranted discipline! What a sad, unfortunate thing it would be for a student to get in trouble when they, in fact, weren't at fault. In such a case, how confused and betrayed must they feel? What distrust of educators must they develop? What resentment? Regretfully, how often has this happened to a student?

Why does it happen? I believe it happens because the investigation of a matter is not easy. Investigations take a lot of time and often can be difficult to unearth. It is easy to make mistakes. It is easy to make false assumptions or to allow bias to overshadow objectivity. Also, students are young. They do not yet know how to advocate for themselves. They are easily manipulated. Often, they don't know how to make sense of situations. Many are intimidated by adults and by authority figures. Many of them are taught not to argue with adults. Many of them have learned that whatever the teacher or principal says, goes. Often, they feel like nothing can reverse the school's verdict on a matter.

Therefore, as a matter of ethics, I implore all educators to tread carefully when working with students through discipline. Respect the need for a thorough investigation—each and every time! Always listen to the student. Consider everything they are saying. Double check their story and the stories of others. When you are certain the student did something, make sure there is enough evidence to nearly guarantee your decision. It is far better to allow a student to get away with wrongdoing than to falsely accuse and discipline the wrong student. Our justice system is based on the belief that everyone is "innocent until proven guilty." It is true that schools have a lesser burden of proof when handling situations than the police or courts have. Legally, only a preponderance of evidence is required in schools. In other words, you need to be more certain than not that something happened or that someone did something. However, in my personal and professional opinion, in order to err on the side of being ethical and just, I have always strived to have near certain proof in a matter. That way, I can go to sleep at night knowing I haven't falsely accused and unjustly disciplined a student. In my career, I feel as certain as possible that I have never falsely accused and then unjustly disciplined a student—never! What I mean is that I am certain I haven't disciplined the wrong person. Certainly, there may have been an instance that I am unaware of, but I hope that is not the case. Imagine how it would feel if it were you—if you were the student! Imagine if it were your child! If we are working with students, we must take this matter seriously. I believe it is a matter of ethics and justice. I trust every educator agrees. The challenge is to make it a priority, knowing that all of us are fallible and prone to bias. In making discipline determinations, I argue that we must be as scrupulous as detectives and as wise and judicial as the court of law. Students deserve such attention to detail and fair treatment.

CHAPTER 2

Relational Discipline

PART I: THE WAY YOU *POSITION* YOURSELF
IN THE RELATIONSHIP

I will never forget the invaluable lessons I learned when working for one season at a juvenile detention facility. Needing to find a job while finishing college, prior to my first teaching position, I applied to work as a detention worker at a nearby juvenile detention facility. I knew of the facility after some of my students during my student teaching assignment were placed there. The initial 1-week training upon employment at the facility was one of the best professional development experiences in my career. I learned a ton of new methods for effectively working with youth and disruptive behaviors. The trainer, who was in charge of the facility, was a former teacher. Once on the job, I continued to learn all kinds of skillful ways to relate to "difficult" youth, ranging from elementary-age students who had been placed in the emotionally disturbed unit to adolescents in the jail (referred to as the lockdown unit).

Much of my learning came from listening to and observing a certain worker, who I'll refer to as Kevin. Kevin was a firefighter who had also worked at the detention facility for over a decade. In stark contrast to Kevin was another worker who I will refer to as Kim. Kim was extremely nurturing. She was in her 50s and had such genuine love for the kids in the facility. However, she lacked resolve. As a result, she was taken advantage of by the kids on a daily basis. I quickly learned to imitate Kevin and do the opposite of Kim!

Kevin *never* raised his voice or yelled at the kids. He was just as kind as Kim. He had great relationships with the kids in detention. The difference between the two of them was that Kevin had an uncanny influence over the kids' behavior, while Kim was treated like a doormat. Kevin would simply *ask* the kids to do something, and they would do it. If they refused, he would very calmly follow through with a fair and clear consequence. Often, he would provide a calm reminder or warning to pick up a piece of paper that was thrown on the floor, for example, and if the kid wouldn't comply, he would have the kid go into their cell for a period of time. If the kid refused, then a higher level consequence would follow. Because kids *knew* Kevin would follow through, never losing his cool, they learned to avoid more severe consequences, such as loss of privileges like gym time. Very seldom would they challenge his requests. Kevin was kind and consistent. Kevin was always clear in his expectations, his words, and his decisions. He was *respected* by the kids in the detention facility.

In contrast, Kim was *liked* by the kids, seemingly more so than Kevin was, but they liked her because of what they could get from her, which was basically whatever they wanted. For example, one time a boy asked Kim if he could put a broom away in a custodial closet that was in a space that separated the boys' and girls' lockdown areas. She couldn't bring herself to say "no." Once allowed, the boy was able to slip into the girls' area, which was a major breach of facility rules. The boy was discovered and received corresponding consequences from the facility. Unfortunately, Kim also got in trouble. This was not the first nor the last time Kim was fooled by the teenagers at the facility. Kids loved to be around Kevin *and* Kim, but for different reasons. With Kevin, kids knew what was expected and they acted accordingly. They enjoyed being around him. Perhaps they felt safe. Boundaries were clear, and when followed, healthy relationships ensued. With Kim, kids knew they could get away with any mischievous desires. Although loving, Kim often appeared frustrated and tired from "chasing" around misbehaving kids. In contrast, Kevin seemed to love coming to work, knowing that his interactions with the kids would be calm, orderly, and as result, enjoyable.

What I learned from watching Kevin was that the way you *position* yourself in the adult-to-youth relationship is paramount. The key is to position yourself as an external force, acting more as a *helper* than an authority trying to control the students. Be someone who clearly outlines fair and clear expectations. Then, allow the students to make their own choices. One of the most trusted experts on child development, Fred Rogers (2019), famous for his many decades as a prized television figure for kids, said, "When a child's urge to be an individual gets channeled into choice-making, it's less likely to go into contrariness" (p. 71).

It's important to encourage, advise, and admonish before students make their own decisions, and also thereafter. But, the key is to *let* students make their *own* choices. As the adult, your job is to clarify the *two paths* set before a young person, constantly reminding them that one path leads to *good* things and the other leads to *bad* things. One path produces healthy and productive outcomes, while the other often leads to more turmoil and negative outcomes. The outcomes ultimately affect the decision-maker, that is, the student! It is their choice to make. When the student chooses the right path, provide praise and allow the natural consequences of good things to come forth. When the student chooses the wrong path, be consistent with predetermined consequences while simultaneously caring for the well-being of the student.

For example, when a teacher is acting too authoritatively, even if doing so out of love, the typical young person sees nothing but the teacher—the authority figure. Developmentally, the student reacts against the power struggle. Instead of seeing the two paths, they see *you*, which antagonizes them in that moment of decision-making. The scenario is perceived by the young person as a "versus" approach. Let me be clear. The adult in this scenario isn't always the power-hungry type. Often, it is the typical adult who is genuinely trying to help the student. Unfortunately, the caring adult has positioned themself in a way that obscures the student's focus on what really matters, which is the presentation of two paths for the young person's decision.

By shifting the way the adult positions themself, the adult becomes subconsciously perceived by the young person as a helper who is focused on guiding the behavioral decision that is to come from the young person. I refer to this positioning as the "relational" approach. It is a non-punitive approach. The young person is able to see the two paths, which are communicated clearly and calmly by the adult and are reinforced by previous standards of consistency. Because the options before the young person are clear, and hopefully perceived to be fair, many young persons will choose the path that brings positive outcomes. Human nature desires good things. Selfishly—in a good sense—the young person will choose the path of least resistance, which should be the good path. However, because they are human, there will be times the young person chooses the wrong path. And that's okay! Through taking the wrong path, they are provided with a different opportunity, an opportunity to experience *accountability*. This accountability will hopefully contribute to better decisions the next time they are presented with the two paths between right and wrong.

The versus approach manifests itself as a "you *and* them" situation. The relational approach is nonpersonal. It's about *them*, not you. The adult removes themself from the power struggle by being calm, clear, and consistent. To the student, the versus approach makes the rules and expectations appear to be *yours*. With the relational approach, the rules and expectations become *theirs*. You hold the power in the versus approach. In the relational approach, the rules (or two paths) hold the power. The student can't change the two paths, but they can change their behavior, choosing the path they want to take. One path promises good outcomes, the other assures undesirable outcomes. The versus approach is about controlling the *student*. The relational approach is about controlling the *situation*. The former is perceived as a *mandate*, while the latter is presented as a *choice*. Both approaches provide an ultimatum. With the versus approach, the ultimatum is, "You *will* do this or that." With the relational approach, the ultimatum is, "*If* you choose this, *then* you will get that." Again, the relational approach is nonpersonal in that the situation is really one between the young person and the two paths they need to decide between. *Telling* occurs in the versus approach. *Explaining* (or *teaching*) occurs in the relational approach. The versus approach tries to *coerce*, while the relational approach seeks to *persuade*.

In *How to Win Friends and Influence People*, Dale Carnegie (1936) asserts:

> You can tell people they are wrong by a look or an intonation or a gesture just as eloquently as you can in words—and if you tell them they are wrong, do you make them want to agree with you? Never! For you have struck a direct blow at their intelligence, judgment, pride and self-respect. That will make them want to strike back. But it will never make them want to change their minds. You may then hurl at them all the logic of a Plato or an Immanuel Kant, but you will not alter their opinions, for you have hurt their feelings. (p. 123)

In avoiding power struggles, Carnegie adds:

> If a man's heart is rankling with discord and ill feeling toward you, you can't win him to your way of thinking with all the logic of Christendom. Scolding parents and domineering bosses and husbands and nagging wives ought to realize that people don't want to change their minds. They can't be forced or driven to agree with you or me. But they may possibly be led to, if we are gentle and friendly, ever so gentle and ever so friendly. (p. 145)

Instead:

> There is only one way under high heaven to get anybody to do anything. Did you ever stop to think of that? Yes, just one way. And that is by making the other person want to do it. (p. 18).

In using the versus approach, most educators are seeking to do the right thing. However, their positionality is unwittingly creating a power struggle. Haberman (1995) writes:

> Teacher strength is an inner quality demonstrated by an ability to share authority with children and youth whom most people are unwilling to trust. (p. 91)

By taking the relational approach, which is to position yourself as a helper who shows the two paths, letting the student make his own choice, educators can find more success with challenging students. Educators can begin to *win* with misbehaving students.

One of the hardest parts with the relational approach is controlling yourself—the adult. It takes a conscious effort to think about the way you are presenting yourself when dealing with a defiant student, or even a student who is displaying subtle misbehavior. For many educators, using the relational approach is as easy as making a slight, yet purposeful shift in the way you present yourself when interacting with the student. It's not too dissimilar from a spouse reminding themself to listen to their partner's perspective before uttering their own stance on a matter. Sometimes, taking a step back from a situation—figuratively speaking—can provide the opportunity for the educator to put on "the relational hat" instead of having a "versus" demeanor. We need to see ourselves "as humans interacting with other humans and not as power figures controlling the behavior of others" (Haberman, 1995, p. 7).

Here are some tips for controlling yourself so that you as the adult don't slip into the versus perception:

Twelve Tips to Maintain a Nonconfrontational Stance

- Always stay calm. Don't raise your voice, show anger, or talk too excitedly.
- Assume nothing. Don't judge. Every student is innocent until proven guilty, so to speak. One of the gravest mistakes

an educator can make is punishing a student who is in fact not responsible for the wrongdoing that is in question. Focus on facts. Let facts guide the conversation, your eventual judgment, and the essence of your resulting decision in providing discipline.

- Let the student explain. Let the student ask questions. Permit the student to vent. The student might need to talk longer than you prefer, and they may bounce from one wild thought to another. They might make their own accusations and say some not-so-nice things, but be patient. The student's outpouring of words provides many benefits. It allows them to release some emotions and thoughts. It can make them feel respected, knowing that the adult cares enough to listen. Also, it can provide the adult with valuable information, helping the adult to have a better understanding of what has happened, where the student's mind and motives are situated, and how to navigate through next steps. However, there may come a time when a student exceeds a standard of civility in their communication. In such cases, the educator can provide a clear and firm reminder that such escalated emotion, which is becoming offensive and unproductive, will need to stop. Often, providing a small break can benefit these kinds of uncivil situations. The adult can simply say, "Lauren, I feel like this is getting a little too heated (or is becoming inappropriate). I'd like for you to step outside (from the office or classroom or a few steps down the hall) so we can both calm down. In a few minutes, when you are ready, we can continue in a calmer manner."
- Be willing to dialogue, even debate with respect. Your goal is to help the student understand; to see things from a different perspective. You shouldn't try to *tell* the student how to act before they are ready to understand. Often, the student will gain a better understanding of the situation and their own actions through the "muddiness" of dialogue and venting utterances.
- To a large extent, time shouldn't be your concern. Sometimes the best dialogues take time. A chance to dialogue and help a student change their behavior is more important than a class period of content. Of course, reflect on whether you as the adult are contributing to unnecessarily long conversations because you are talking too much or you haven't learned how

to guide a student's venting. Observing a glassed-over look or blank stare on the student's face is usually a tell-tale sign!

- Don't nag, harp on a topic, belabor a point, or show frustration.
- Don't "hold a student hostage" by lecturing the student about life lessons if the student is completely unwilling to listen or dialogue.
- Don't be offended by eye rolling, lack of eye contact, an occasional curse word, anger at the situation, disagreement, pouting, "woe is me" talk, or even refusal to listen and/or understand. These are often natural (and expected!) characteristics of their age and development. Don't let these sort of emotional and developmentally normal behaviors disrupt you from your ultimate goal, which is to *help* the student gain awareness of both self and situation, thereby accepting responsibility (or accountability) for their actions and/or influencing their decision to choose the right path.
- If you make an attempt to speak "the hard truth," do so in love. Anytime you say something that is hard for someone to hear, or is a potential attack on their identity, or is seen as a lecture on life, make sure they are ready and willing to "have ears to hear." Making this judgment is an art. You will have a sense of when you can and when you can't "go there," and whom you can and can't go there with. Some adults are really skilled at saying the hard truth in a way that productively influences others. With some other adults it backfires and is a practice that should be avoided.
- If you raise your voice or exert unusual firmness, make sure it is purposeful for that unique moment and set of circumstances. Sometimes, this approach can powerfully and productively impact a student. However, it is an artful approach that should only be reserved for particular moments when the adult feels confident that it is what the student needs at that moment. Although it is not any kind of science, a helpful concept is to recognize that sometimes a calm student can be receptive to a contrasting voice of firmness and power, while an emotionally escalated student almost always needs to be countered with a calm demeanor. Somehow, we as humans seem to ebb and flow with one another in such a manner. In other words, two yelling voices rarely find harmony.
- When issuing discipline, always explain the rationale for the consequence. Also, articulate what the future will look

like for the student after they move forward and serve the consequence. This is your opportunity to help them see a longer and broader vision of their life and the impact of their decisions and behaviors. It is your chance to impart the wisdom that you as an adult have gained, knowing that they are in the process of learning such wisdom. This can provide the student with a sense of hope. It can remind the student that the point of discipline is to teach, to learn, to grow, and to become better.

- Don't be discouraged if a student presents a posture of being bored or is intent on making it appear as though they are not listening. Of course, sometimes they aren't listening and the adult needs to recognize this. But, be reminded that often kids haven't yet gained the social skill or awareness to make eye contact or show respect when having difficult conversations. Eye contact may also be considered disrespectful in their culture. Also, humans rarely want to admit to being wrong in the midst of confrontation. One thing I have learned over the years when working with students is that they *do* listen to adults more than they make it seem. As educators, we need to become accustomed to the blank stares and straight faces that our students wield our way. As previously mentioned, this is developmentally normal, just as it is developmentally normal for young people to seek wisdom from adults.

PART II: THE *WORDS* YOU CHOOSE TO USE

In addition to the way you position yourself in the adult-to-student relationship, the equally important component to relational discipline is the art of how you speak. The actual words you choose to use in discipline situations can determine enormously how successful you will be in persuading a student to choose one path over another. At first, the practice of *word choice*, or what I sometimes call *speech control*, will seem contrived and somewhat robotic. It may feel unnatural. But, by committing to this practice, it will become a habit and will improve over time.

I remember when I was newly married my wife said to me, "Adam, sometimes it's *what* you say that actually matters." We all have heard that *how* you say something matters. But, my wife was communicating to me that *what* we say matters, too. I had created the habit of asking when she came home, "How's it going?" or "How are you?" Over time, she told me that my questioning seemed generic. It didn't seem authentic. Bewildered (and newly wedded!), I complained, "Well, what should I ask?" She responded, "I want you to sometimes ask, 'How are you *feeling?*'" I thought, what's the difference? Having realized that it wasn't worth debating, I said that I would try to work on it. Throughout the years it has actually become a running joke in our marriage when I ask her, with exaggerated intonation, "How are you *feeeeeling* today?" Nonetheless, this helped me learn that words do matter. Even if it seems silly and unlikely, for whatever reason a different selection of words in a given situation can change everything when it comes to the dynamics of human interaction—especially in contentious and challenging moments.

I love the title of Andrea Gardner's (2012) book *Change Your Words, Change Your World.* I'm not sure just when I learned this approach as an educator, but through doing the regular work of being with students, I came to realize the power of word choice and speech control. I began making it a habit, and now there are many phrases I use with students, especially in discipline situations, that promise good results. Some of these phrases just work! Especially coupled with the relational approach of how you position yourself, the words you use can make all of the difference in persuading a student. Certain words and phrases carry a better tune than others. Something in our brain finds harmony with one set of words over another set. The more I sharpen my skill in this, the more phrases I develop. Some educators will succeed with some of these phrases, while others will make adjustments to which words they use. Different personalities will find some that work for them and others that don't. The important thing is to recognize the power of using certain words and phrases for certain situations, then through trial and error discover which ones appear to soften the tension and calm the turmoil in contentious discipline situations or conversations.

Below are a list of words and phrases that I use and have found to be successful when working with students in discipline situations and conversations. I insert them at apropos moments in my conversations with students. Hopefully you will notice how nicely these phrases mesh with the "helper" positionality that was explained in the previous section. Please understand that none of these phrases are to be said in a condescending or patronizing tone, nor are they to be said with aggressive or overly authoritative inflection. Rather, they are to be said with sincerity, albeit at times, still in a firm manner.

- "I'm for you, not against you."
- "My job is to be a helper to you."
- "This is my advice. You can take it or leave it." (This is said in a caring, non-abrupt way).
- "I'm *asking* you to. . . ."
- "You can keep acting this way, but you are just going to keep running into walls in life. It's your life and you can do what you want. I'm trying to help you so you don't have to do that."
- "Please don't talk that way to me (or in here). I will always treat you with respect, but I expect the same from you."
- "I'm not mad. I don't get mad." (This is a lie of course! But, it helps communicate your objective guidance. Also, it helps you to remain calm).
- "This is how I see life, both for you and for me—for all people: If you make good choices, good things typically happen. If you make bad choices, bad things typically happen. It's your choice."
- "In life there are usually two paths: A good one and a not-so-good one. You can go down either path. It's your choice."
- "Even if my own child were to do this (that is, what the student did), I'd have to move forward with a consequence because doing so is important. Doing so is, in fact, ethical."
- "I can't *not* get you in trouble. Upholding a standard of behavior for this school (or this classroom) is essential, even ethical."
- "You're not in charge. In fact, I'm not in charge. Someone's in charge of me, too. You have to follow rules. I have to follow rules. It will be this way your whole life."
- "I'm going to give you discipline, but my hope is that you will take responsibility for your actions, serve the consequence, and then move on by putting this in your past (or by having this be the last time you make this choice or act this way)."
- "If we could redo this situation, what could you have done differently?" (Sometimes a student can benefit from you telling them how they could have behaved instead or what choice they could have made instead. They might not know unless you provide them with the wisdom that they have not yet gained.)

Although these words and phrases, and this speech control approach in general, may seem overly simple and perhaps dubious, I recommend that educators try them. I am hopeful that you will be pleasantly surprised and will begin to sharpen your own speech control, using particular words and phrases that work for you and your students. Sometimes, particular students and unique situations require a different set of speech control. Below are some words and phrases that are tailored for atypical moments.

Explosive Students

- When making a command, get appropriately close to the student, make eye contact, display soft, non-threatening body language, speak calmly, and with respect say, "Can you please (do this or that)?" If they refuse, say, "I need for you to (do this or that)." If they still refuse, say, "I'm going to give you one more chance. I've treated you with respect, and if you don't do what I ask, then there will be a consequence." Sometimes with really defiant students, it can be effective to also tell them that you are going to walk away and come back in a few minutes. At that point they will need to be prepared to either comply or receive a consequence. If they *still* refuse, say, "I need for you to go (somewhere such as outside the office, or if in a classroom, then into the hallway)," and then in the meantime decide on a consequence. You don't have to tell them what the consequence is right there on the spot. Often because of your consistency with expectations and consequences, they may already know. If they don't know, they can know moments later. There is no need to "poke the bear" by making the known consequence the new center of attention, leading to a larger disruption.
- Sometimes you can surprise them by getting to the root of the matter by asking, "Is there something else going on?" I've had students suddenly open up about something traumatic in their home life, which allows us to talk about the root issue that is driving their misbehavior.
- "What is it that you are mad about?"
- "Do you need a minute (to yourself)?"
- "You cannot act this way in here. I'm willing to give you a moment to yourself to cool down, but I expect that once you are done you will act reasonably."
- If a student tries to make a scene in front of other students during a power struggle, often it can be effective to communicate that there will be a consequence for their

actions, telling them that you will let them know what it is after class (or when no one else is around). By doing this, the other students see that you have the situation under control, that the student will be held accountable, but there is no need to continue the power struggle for the moment. Then, you as the educator should return your attention back to the other students, continuing whatever task you had been working on. As an administrator, I've even done this in the lunch room or the hallways in front of nearly a hundred students in an attempt to uphold the standard of accountability, while not "poking the bear" and making the situation worse. Of course, this approach is not necessarily recommended in dangerous situations or with students who can in a moment become a threat to themselves or others.

Continually Stubborn Students

- Always use a sensitive and calm, yet straightforward, tone of voice.
- "That's fine (since the student has made his choice and isn't appearing to budge). I hope you make the right choice."
- "If you don't want my advice and you don't want my help, that's fine. That's your choice and I will respect that. We can end this conversation. If you change your mind, you know where to find me."
- "Jason, I like you. You may not think that, but I really do." Often, stubborn and defiant students need to hear this in no uncertain language. In fact, it might be the reason why they are misbehaving—to get attention and see if anyone even cares.
- Tell the student the consequence their actions deserve, then provide them with unexpected mercy, informing them that you have decided this one time that you are going to forgo discipline. I've had very stubborn students, who being totally shocked by this act of grace, have not known what to do with the power struggle they have created other than to completely soften and engage in dialogue for the first time. Some people might think this is inconsistent. Certainly it can be if used too often or not handled with care. However, as a consistent educator, you will have likely gained such a reputation of being fair and clear that an occasional second chance will have no negative impact on your professionalism. Even courts in the

justice system reserve the right to issue probation instead of punishment. If you need an official justification or some kind of documentation, the decision can be treated as an official warning, or written into a deferral agreement or placed in abeyance similar to what is done in many expulsion hearings.

- Sometimes an effective strategy can be to tell the student that they deserve a certain consequence, but since you don't want to see them go down that path, you are going to call their parent (if you are an administrator, you can do this on the spot in your office while the student sits across from you) and ask the parent to talk to the student. Then, actually call the parent, explain that the student deserves a certain consequence (actually tell them what it is) because of what they did (explain it to the parent). Then, tell the parent that you would like to give the student one more chance and that you are asking the parent to please speak with the student to help the student change their mind—to comply. Amazingly, I've found this strategy to work with some of the most defiant students and I've received enormous support from their parents—even from parents who aren't always supportive!

Emotional Students or Students Overwhelmed by Guilt

- "Listen to me. You *will* get past this. Life will go on. You can learn from this and be better off because of it."
- Play the fool by sharing a story from your own life, about what once happened to you when you also messed up. Intrinsically, youth respect educators. They see educators as role models who have figured out life (even though we know this isn't true!). Take advantage of your position as a role model to show your vulnerable side. In doing so, they might be able to see themselves in you. They might be able to think, "Hey, even Ms. K. made mistakes, and now look at her! Look at what she has become!" Playing the fool, as I like to say, can be a very powerful tool to inspire others.
- "Trust me. Everything's going to be okay. I promise."
- Recognize that an emotional student is often experiencing some level of anxiety. By helping them see a larger picture and gain a broader perspective, the anxiety can often be reduced.
- With students who tend to be obsessive or can become fixated on certain thoughts, sometimes switching their attention to

something completely separate (like a piece of candy, a new topic completely unrelated, or another distraction) can break the cycle in their minds. I've had some students literally forget the topic they had been obsessing over, creating a mental restart.

SUMMARY: RELATIONAL DISCIPLINE

Relational discipline that is non-punitive is not just a matter of caring for students (although, of course, any educator who effectively relates to students must care). Specifically, relational discipline is a skill. It is a competency that can be mastered. It is an art form that can through continual use and refinement become a kind of science. In other words, it can become so habitual and effective that it yields predictable results in working with misbehaving students. Relational discipline requires a shift in one's mindset. The educator's position shifts from a "versus" approach to a relational approach. The positionality deals with how the educator is perceived by the student in the moment of confrontation. The educator maintains authority, but the focus shifts from a power struggle to a clear presentation of the two paths set before the student. Through clear, calm, and caring language, the educator helps the developing young person see more clearly the options before them. Then, relational discipline utilizes word choice and speech control to guide the student down the right path. Power struggles are calmed, distractions are removed, and clarity is opened for the young person. The educator facilitates the process of student choice. The educator presents themself as the student's helper. With time and practice, any educator can begin to master relational discipline and can begin to *win* with misbehaving students, helping them to make better choices. If you are continually battling with a student, then either you are caught up in some kind of power or ego struggle or you are trying to be Superman by trying to "fix" a person who is not willing or ready to change. Instead, through the practice of relational discipline, accept that you can't control anyone—you can only try your best, blaze a path for the student, and endlessly encourage them to walk down it. Relational discipline is the key to knowing how to *win* with misbehaving students!

CHAPTER 3

Misconceptions

MISCONCEPTION 1: IT'S ONE EXTREME OR THE OTHER

In many situations, we find ourselves on one end of a spectrum. Perhaps it's human nature. Often we see things in black and white. For whatever reasons, we allow ourselves to forget that variations of gray and a myriad of exceptions surround and constitute most situations in life. We realize it later when we encounter new experiences that shift our way of thinking. A young person might say, I will *never* do that when I'm married or when I raise a child. Once married or when parenting, he finds himself behaving exactly as he swore never to behave. Meanwhile, his elders respectfully laugh, knowing that with time he would learn on his own. Most situations aren't simple. Usually, we find the best solutions somewhere in the middle between two extremes.

When it comes to the topic of discipline in education, we often debate between the extremes of punishment and light reprimands. When a student breaks a rule or wrongs someone, one emotional response is to punish the perpetrator. We often say, "They need a consequence!" In this tone, a consequence equates to some type of punishment—something that will hurt. If it doesn't hurt—so the logic goes—then the child will not learn from their mistake. The consequence must be properly painful. Just as a young toddler won't touch a hot stove a second time, so also will the suffering student avoid future folly. However, we know this is an extreme stance and isn't always true. Sometimes it is true. Many times it isn't. Again, negative consequences do not guarantee a change in student behavior—in fact, they may make some situations worse!

The other extreme is to simply reprimand the misbehaving student. Rather than to enact a concrete action, such as a detention or suspension, to just provide a verbal rebuke. There is no doubt that this approach is easier than the other extreme. Mere words are all that are needed. Many people have found success in providing a clear and meaningful reprimand. Others have mastered the ability to speak with such care and concern that the student can't help but change his behavior. However, there is no guarantee that this approach is any more effective than its counterpart at the other side of the disciplinary spectrum.

Why do we in education find ourselves arguing between these two extremes? If we step back from a particular situation, from our emotions, and from our default mindsets, can't we agree that the best approach is easily somewhere in the middle? I suggest that the answer is akin to our ideal image of good parenting. A good parent disciplines their children. This is something we know to be honorable and for the future benefit of the children. However, we equally know that the discipline must be done in love. After a timeout, there will be a "moving on" that will occur—no grudge, no hard feelings. Conversely, what parent hasn't withheld a warranted punishment when they feel a reprimand for that moment will suffice?

In my own life as a parent, there was a time when my son knew he deserved a certain consequence for the action he chose. He made a really bad decision that warranted a really bad consequence. He knew the consequence was coming. Prior to his wrongdoing, I couldn't have been clearer about what the consequence would be. Nonetheless, when I went to deliver the consequence, he trembled with such regret and genuine sorrow that I decided mercy would teach him better than punishment. Being shocked and relieved by mercy, he became even more vulnerable and humble. In that moment, he melted in my arms and apologized with raw sincerity. I believe he learned more from that display of mercy than he would have from a negative consequence. Had I sworn to follow through with a punishment *no matter what,* then I would have missed the opportunity to create more lasting change in his behavior. On the other hand, I must admit that there have been many times I have failed my children by *not* following through with a consequence. By being inconsistent, I have at times taught my children that they can get away with certain behaviors.

The misconception here is that we need to take one extreme over the other. Each situation calls for wisdom and action that is *appropriate* for that moment and for that particular child. Most situations will necessitate a balance between being firm and forgiving. If we lack either, we will likely fail in our effort to improve student behavior. That deserves repeating: If we lack *either,* we will likely fail in our effort to improve youth behavior.

MISCONCEPTION 2: RULES SHOULD BE STATED
IN THE POSITIVE

Although I agree that many rules are better worded when stated in the positive, I contend that this should not become an absolute creed. Whether a rule is positive or negative is not the point. Rather, what matters is that rules and expectations are *fair* and *clear.* For example, "Thou shall not murder!" That is a negative statement, yet it is profoundly just and abundantly clear. Why should it be said any other way? Puppies are told, "Don't bite." Parents must say "no" to many of their kids' requests. A loving mother might be heard saying to her child in a loud voice, "Stop" or "Stop that!" What matters most is that the rules and expectations are fair and clear. I would argue that some rules are more clear when they *are* stated in the negative. One of my classroom mantras was, "Since I care about each and every student's academic success, I will *not* allow students to behave in any manner that disrupts student learning or the classroom teaching." I wanted this expectation to be said exactly like that. I wanted it to have a negative tone because in being negative, it carried more emotion. I felt that it communicated a level of seriousness. I wanted to communicate that student learning was so important that I wouldn't—that I couldn't—allow anything to get in its way. This mantra was very clear and it reflected the primary goal of schooling—student learning.

Therefore, I encourage teachers not to worry about whether or not their rules and expectations are stated in the positive or negative, but to focus on if they are *fair* and *clear.* The goal is to teach and reinforce appropriate boundaries. Within those boundaries, students will have many positive opportunities to flourish. According to Fred Rogers (2019):

> Providing a framework doesn't take away children's individuality. In fact, structure generally helps them to be more free because it provides boundaries. It's like a fence that offers security for what can happen inside the enclosure. Respect flourishes best within a *clear* [emphasis added] framework, and it's that framework that can allow us all to express more of who we really are. (p. 75)

Furthermore, a few fair and clear rules, even if stated in the negative, will have no negative impact on a classroom environment that is full of good instruction, genuine respect, appropriate fun, and caring hearts!

In fact, such rules may help to quicken the students' understanding of boundaries so that meaningful learning can take priority sooner rather than later.

MISCONCEPTION 3: ONE SIZE FITS ALL

Consistency in a school building is important. In fact, many of the strategies that are provided elsewhere in this book are predicated on the importance of consistency. Frameworks can be very helpful in merging a wide range of mindsets and opinions. A good school culture can help solidify common approaches that benefit students. However, when it comes to student discipline, we must remember that "one size doesn't fit all." Controversy can arise within schools when teachers disagree about discipline practices. A teacher might complain, "It's not fair that students don't get in trouble in Ms. P.'s class; it makes me look like the bad guy when I follow through with discipline and she doesn't." Often, teachers might disagree with a discipline decision made by the administration. Someone might say, "I can't believe the principal didn't deal with that student," when the student received a consequence less than a suspension, for example.

Here's what I would ask educators: Do all families agree on how to discipline their children? Don't you know of families who raised well-adjusted children by being strict or even in some cases harsh? Don't you know of other families who raised equally well-adjusted kids by being lenient? Do you discipline and raise your children exactly how you were disciplined and raised? Do your neighbors, who also have great kids, discipline exactly how you discipline? Here's an even tougher question: Don't you even discipline your own children differently from one another from time to time, based on specific situations and with a mindfulness toward the differences in your children's personalities?

In raising my own children, my son required different discipline than was required by my daughter. They have very different personalities. Often, my son needed a stern and unpleasant consequence. On the other hand, my daughter could melt from one look or admit fault through a meaningful conversation. If there is so much variance in parenting styles, then why do we expect all educators to discipline the same way?

Instead of pursuing a one-size-fits-all approach, schools should focus on two principles that should earmark every discipline situation:

Address the misbehavior and seek *growth* from it. Addressing student behavior deals with *accountability*. Accountability is much more important than obsessing or arguing over the exact consequence, and it is certainly more educative than punishment. We fail students (or our own children) when we dismiss or ignore behaviors that violate healthy boundaries and hinder personal or community growth. Matters need to be addressed. *How* we address them can vary. Perhaps they should vary depending on the personality of the adult, the emotions of the child, and the details surrounding a particular situation. Again, Rogers (2019) suggests:

> The appropriateness of a punishment depends on the unique personality and experiences of each individual parent and each child, and, above all, on the unique quality of the relationship between them. (p. 74)

Some situations warrant a detention, others a suspension. Some situations may warrant restitution. Others may need only a conversation. All situations need restoration. As mentioned before, some situations may benefit from unexpected mercy. However, in all of these circumstances, the misbehavior is *addressed.* Addressing student misbehavior reinforces the concept of *accountability* for the student's actions.

In addition, all discipline situations should involve *growth*. If a student grows through a painful consequence, then great! In the adult world, a prison sentence could be an example of a fair and ultimately beneficial experience if the individual learns from the consequence. I've known many students who have learned, accepted responsibility, and changed their behavior *because of* a suspension from school. I've known many others who learned nothing from a suspension; rather, the consequence was received as a desirable vacation! We want the student to learn from his mistakes. The very word "discipline" implies learning—becoming a disciple of a better way of living. If school discipline isn't meant to foster growth, then we are working for something other than the welfare of children.

This line of thinking brings me to the use of the word "punishment." The topic of discipline includes certain words that invoke a variety of connotations. Sometimes, a word holds polar opposite meanings for two individuals who, in reality, hold very similar perspectives. For example, the word "punishment," when used, can be very misleading. A teacher might say, "Jason needs to be punished for what he did!" Another teacher might respond, "Punished? Discipline should teach the student, helping him to change. It's about growth, not punishment!"

In this example, we need to know what the former teacher *meant* by "punishment." The teacher might have meant exactly what was said by the latter teacher. If he did, then both teachers share the same perspective. The difference is that one teacher is more comfortable with using the word "punishment," while the other loathes the word. However, if the former teacher uses the word "punishment," but desires suffering, then he does conceptualize discipline in a much different way than the other teacher.

Another loaded word can be "discipline." When some educators say, "Megan needs to be disciplined," they expect an action to be taken in the form of a concrete consequence, such as a detention. However, other teachers perceive discipline to have occurred when the misbehavior is *addressed*. Therefore, the teachers who want the situation addressed, might be fine with a verbal reprimand. To them, that is still "discipline." To the other teachers, a verbal reprimand is anything but discipline.

As a result, how do we navigate the misleading interpretations that stem from these semantics? Essentially, schools need to improve their conversations about many of the loaded words that are used when talking about discipline. Educators need to do a better job of communicating with one another and with school administration. If a teacher says to their principal, "I think Megan needs to be disciplined," the principal should explicitly ask, "What are you thinking; what do you think is a good consequence?" Also, a principal could take the time to talk with a teacher and share, "Ms. M, I'm wondering if the student is willing to apologize. If they are willing, are you okay with that being the conclusion to this matter or do you think further action is necessary?" We can remind one another by saying things like, "Remember, our goal here is to see a change in behavior. What do you think can help bring about a change with this student?" Communication solves a lot of problems and clarifies a lot of misunderstanding!

MISCONCEPTION 4: DISCIPLINE IS ENOUGH

I am aware that some who read this book might at times get the feeling that I'm discouraging discipline and promoting instead a mantra that believes relationships alone will fix every situation. It is correct that I *am* promoting the importance of relationships when working with students, especially when using some of the strategic approaches and resources that I have found to work within my own career. However,

I fully support the use of school discipline—actually, I believe it is essential. Much of this book seeks to *shift* the emphasis from discipline as a stand-alone product to discipline within the *skillful* practice of a purposeful relationship (i.e., *relational discipline*). Part of my aim is to help educators think about discipline *differently*. The goal is to help educators to *shift* how they position themselves with their students, becoming savvier in how they administer discipline while maintaining a positive relationship with their students. As you will read with the next misconception, I believe suspensions and even expulsions are still necessary in schools. Every student needs to learn boundaries and must be held accountable. Educators should be firm, clear, and consistent (again, you can be all of these things while still being fair, kind, and gentle).

Therefore, yes, discipline is necessary! It absolutely is. But, discipline alone is not enough. I've come to a point where I try to think about every discipline situation in the following way: Discipline *and what?* Never should we *just* think about issuing discipline. Never should we administer discipline with nothing to follow or accompany it. Discipline should be married to some kind of *next step*; some kind of support mechanism to foster growth. This is akin to restorative practices. To find the balance between *accountability* and *growth*. To find the balance between the need for *discipline* and *relationship*.

Let's look at a classic scenario. A student breaks a classroom rule and based on the teacher's discipline plan, they receive a detention or are referred to the principal's office. Okay, good. The teacher has followed through with discipline. The teacher is being firm, clear, and consistent. The teacher is holding the student accountable for *their* (the student's) actions and is *implicitly* reinforcing the need to respect behavioral boundaries. It's easy to stop there. However, if the educator stops at this point, they are assuming that the discipline alone is enough, and rarely is it. Accompanying the consequence, the student needs to receive some kind of *explicit* teaching. The student needs some kind of *learning* element. In this scenario, the teacher should assign the detention *and what?* The teacher could assign the detention *and* require the student to talk with the teacher during the detention about their behavior—the root causes, lessons learned, and/or how to make better choices in the future. If the teacher can't speak with the student during the detention, the teacher can make a point to debrief with the student the next day or after class.

Another option is for the teacher to assign a consequence *and* then have the student complete a reflection form that facilitates the same kind of questions that would typically occur in a person-to-person meeting. Often, the consequence isn't going to change the student. Actually, it might cause the student to become angry and bitter, leading to more misbehavior. Should the teacher, therefore, withhold discipline? No! The teacher should be firm, clear, and consistent, provide the discipline *and* provide an avenue for additional learning. The teacher might assign the consequence and provide a path to *remedy* the violation. For example, the teacher could assign the detention and provide an opportunity to revoke the detention (or place it in abeyance) *if* the student agrees to take the path to remedy the violation. The path to remedy could be an apology letter, the completion of a reflection form, or a mediation with the teacher, another student, or the class (if the violation affected others). The path to remedy could be some kind of restitution.

Along these lines, a great restorative approach is to use "in lieu of" approaches. An "in lieu of" approach is when you issue discipline, but it can be *reduced*, and in some cases *replaced*, by doing X, Y, or Z. With the vaping epidemic, we instituted this in my school. The results were incredibly successful. At one school, a student received an automatic 6-day suspension for vaping. If after 3 days of suspension, they took an online course that explained the dangers of nicotine and vaping (which we purchased from an outside company), then their suspension was reduced to 3 days and they returned to class after completing the course. Suspensions were thus automatically cut in half. At another school, we implemented the same approach, but the suspension was reduced from 3 days to a day. Students were held accountable—that is, they received discipline—but they were given a chance to reduce the discipline by agreeing to participate in a learning opportunity. This is the true definition of a "win-win" scenario.

Another element to "discipline and what?" is appropriate accommodations in the aftermath of discipline. Both schools and classrooms can make environmental changes after the discipline. The changes are meant to assist the student by modifying or accommodating their current behavioral tendencies. For example, the student received discipline *and* will now have a different seat in the classroom. If the violation happened in the lunchroom, the student could receive discipline *and* be placed in a restricted lunch area until their behavior improves. After the discipline, the student could have a mandatory meeting to discuss a new behavior plan. These interventions are not meant to be punitive. They are meant to help the student avoid future behavioral mistakes. Behavior plans are meant to support the student.

The point is for educators to remember that students will rarely change their behavior *just* from being disciplined. Something else must come with or after the discipline. Often, a simple conversation or meeting will suffice. Senge et al. (2012) assert:

> Schools that train people only to obey authority and follow the rules unquestioningly have poorly prepared their students for our increasingly complex and interdependent world. (p. 7)

We must remember that students, to varying degrees, will misbehave from time to time. It's part of their development and it's part of being human. "Disrespectful behavior often comes down to kids having poor problem-solving skills and a lack of knowledge about how to be more respectful" (Lehman, n.d., para. 9). Haberman (1995) says, "[Star teachers] assume problems are the reason for needing skilled practitioners" (p. 4). As educators, we must prioritize the students' *growth* through the discipline process. "Love, I feel quite certain, is at the root of all *healthy* [emphasis added] discipline" (Rogers, 2019, p. 82).

MISCONCEPTION 5: SUSPENSIONS ARE NOT EFFECTIVE

Suspensions have become a hot topic in the press and among legislators. This is largely because there is little evidence to support the effectiveness of suspensions for *most* students, especially students who are the most at risk of not graduating from high school. Based on a study from the Center for Civil Rights Remedies at the UCLA Civil Rights Project and the Learning Policy Institute, "which analyzed federal data from the 2015–16 school year for nearly every school district in the country," *U.S. News* reports, "Students missed out on 11 million instructional days due to out-of-school suspensions in a single academic year" (Camera, 2020, para. 1). The same study also found that the rates of lost instruction from suspensions for Black students and other students of color are significantly higher than those of White students (Camera, 2020).

It has become common knowledge that suspensions from school can be a pipeline to prison, meaning that suspension rates can be a predictor of future rule-breaking. The school-to-prison pipeline concept suggests that negative consequences are not changing the behavior of certain youth who continue unwanted behavior until they eventually are incarcerated. Flannery (2015) states:

For those students, it isn't just an interruption in learning, although it's definitely that, too—if they aren't in school, they aren't learning. A suspension can be life-altering. It is the number-one predictor—more than poverty—of whether children will drop out of school, and walk down a road that includes greater likelihood of unemployment, reliance on social-welfare programs, and imprisonment. (para. 5)

If suspensions from school aren't changing a student's behavior, then we need to explore alternative approaches for that particular student—remember, "one size doesn't fit all."

However, I disagree that we should abandon suspensions altogether. I disagree that suspensions are always bad. Suspensions can communicate a very important lesson in upholding essential standards for the school environment. In many ways, a suspension communicates that the student's action was and is so disruptive and/or detrimental to the school environment that removal is the appropriate consequence. Suspensions, and discipline in general, can help a student become conscious of what isn't acceptable. In theory, it is analogous to removing a child from a family event because they refuse to be civil, sending a child away from the dinner table because they will not stop throwing food, or removing a football player from a game because of a dirty and dangerous hit on another player. Also, suspensions are similar to jail or prison in the justice system. Of course we don't want to imprison people for the mere sake of it. But certain behaviors deserve a consequence that *separates* an individual from a certain setting. The length of separation must correspond with the magnitude of the offense. Some criminal behaviors result in fines, probation, restitution, community service, or other mediating options. Other criminal behaviors result in jail time. Significant violations result in prison. Some crimes result in a separation from the general population for a year, others for many years, and the most severe even for life! Again, I'm providing an analogy. I'm not suggesting that students are committing crimes. However, schools also must decide what behaviors warrant a separation (i.e., suspension and in some cases expulsion) from the general population (i.e., school).

In a very serious way, suspensions reinforce the boundaries that *must* exist in schools for schools to be safe, orderly, and educative environments. "Happy and healthy family life depends on limits, some that keep family life moving on schedule, others that serve to protect privacy and property" (Rogers, 2019, p. 72). Limits are equally necessary in schools. Although suspensions may not be appropriate for behaviors that don't hinder "moving on schedule," when in-school disciplinary options are more suitable, they sometimes are necessary to protect the remaining community from actions that jeopardize essential rights and matters of safety.

Perhaps the student doesn't learn from the suspension. Perhaps they even enjoy the removal from school since they are allowed to do whatever they want when they're at home. Nonetheless, the student and his family, as well as the remaining school culture, are reminded that certain behaviors will not be tolerated. Suspensions are one of the most severe ways that schools *address* certain behaviors. Some students learn from suspensions and become better; others learn very little and become further damaged by them. Either way, schools can't compromise certain boundaries, which are necessary for the operation of a safe and orderly environment.

I do believe, however, in terms of *growth*, suspensions should be issued with great caution. Suspensions should be preserved for misbehaviors that truly endanger the learning environment. Examples include possession/use/sale of drugs, fighting and violent behaviors, criminal acts, and severe disruption. And when suspensions are issued, educative avenues and resources should accompany them. This is the "*and what?*" concept. Drug violations should include mentoring, counseling, and/or external assistance from experts. Fighting and violent behaviors should include appropriate accommodations upon the student's return and when possible healthy restitution. Severe disruptions should result in new strategies to curtail or avoid certain behaviors, situations, and/or triggers. All suspensions should involve healthy adult-to-student conversations and mentoring—both when issuing the suspension and thereafter. If a student has been suspended multiple times, then educators and the family need to explore alternative options. Such options might involve school accommodations, additional resources/assistance, alternative education placement, or other behavioral strategies. If a student doesn't learn from his suspension and repeats an unacceptable behavior, warranting another suspension, then the school should pause and begin to explore alternative discipline options. Again, the discipline options should focus on growth—on changing the student's behavior. Perhaps the student needs a major change to his educational placement. Perhaps he needs strategic support from the school and/or external agencies.

Although I believe that suspensions *do* have a proper role in schools, I equally believe that they should not be *overused*. Schools need to be cognizant of the disparities that can exist among races and that marginalized students shouldn't receive more suspensions or heavier punishment. Bias exists in all of us and in all of the institutions we are a part of—including schools! Educators and the systems we are a part of must examine our biases and work toward equity so that *every* child is treated with the utmost care

Additionally, educators need to reflect on what student behaviors truly warrant a suspension. Some instances may seem disruptive, but can be handled with an array of alternative consequences. Furthermore, some of these "disruptive" student behaviors can quickly be mitigated and resolved, even prevented, through a relational approach from a skilled practitioner. Such an approach is the essence of this book.

An increasingly popular opinion is that students should not be penalized academically when they are suspended or because they are suspended. Many years ago, there was an attitude among some educators that receiving zero credit on school work during a suspension was part of the duly received "punishment." In fact, very often when I call parents to inform them of a suspension, they automatically assume their child will not be allowed to complete and turn in his schoolwork. At the schools where I have worked, students *are* allowed to complete and submit their schoolwork during and even after their suspension. In fact, they are encouraged to work on their schoolwork during the suspension. Some people reading this might argue, "What's the point, then, of issuing a suspension—the student is getting a free vacation from school with no academic penalty?" My response to the part about no academic penalty: Exactly! The suspension deals with the student's behavior, not his academics. Also, as has been mentioned in this section of this book, suspensions don't guarantee change in the student's behavior. Instead, the suspensions uphold certain standards of what *can't* be tolerated in a school setting. They communicate essential boundaries. A student might prefer a suspension in their effort to avoid school. That's fine. The school must still enforce certain standards and expectations of behavior. However, if the student continues to repeat a behavior that leads to additional suspensions, then at that point in time, the school should examine alternative interventions to address the student's choices.

Therefore, are suspensions ineffective? For most students in America, perhaps they are, but the exceptions are important. That is because there are other systemic, societal issues (e.g., poverty, family life, trauma) that need to be addressed before a school can witness positive results from any suspension. For example, a student who feels marginalized at school and has no consequences at home may in fact enjoy the suspension. But, when students feel connected to their school environment and the potential it offers for their future, then a suspension may deter certain behaviors. Similarly, when parents reinforce expectations from the school and enforce their own consequences at home for receiving a suspension, then students may begin to reflect on their own behaviors. However, individual schools that know their student population and have a keen sense of essential behavioral boundaries that are clearly outlined and communicated, suspensions and even expulsions—or rather, the possibility of each—need to exist as a disciplinary option. If for nothing else, suspensions uphold and communicate essential boundaries necessary for school safety and order. This is also why suspensions should be reserved for exactly such circumstances and not for lessor behaviors that educators can learn to be skilled at curtailing.

MISCONCEPTION 6: ALWAYS FOLLOW THROUGH WITH A CONSEQUENCE

There is no question that being consistent and following through on what you have said or what you have promised is essential to good leadership, especially as it relates to working with young people. Following through with discipline can be difficult. It takes resolve. Before the adult issues discipline, they must have a clear philosophical understanding of what is and isn't permissible, when such a standard exists, and how any form of discretion, if applied, can be justified. Rogers (2019) believes:

> We're afraid we'll lose the love of our children when we don't let them have their way. So we parents need to try to find the security within ourselves to accept the fact that we and our children won't always like one another's actions, that there will be times when we and our children won't be able to be "friends," and that there will be times of real anger. (p. 82)

However, once you begin to think of "following through" as being a matter of taking *action* instead of feeling the need to issue a traditional consequence all the time, you will begin to understand consistency of action in a different way. Yes, with every situation be consistent. But, be consistent by taking action—by doing *something*. In other words, when a student misbehaves, don't do *nothing*. It's important to understand that doing something doesn't always require a punitive consequence. As previously mentioned, the important thing is to *address* misbehavior so that students are held *accountable* in an effort to help them *grow* from the experience. Doing something (or taking action) can come in the form of a warning or a conversation. Some people might scoff at this approach since it doesn't "hurt" the student, but such an opinion is missing the entire point of this book. In some situations, providing a negative consequence could actually drive some students into more rebellion and hinder future growth. Should such students be excused from consequences? In some cases, maybe. But, should they be excused from accountability? Never. In a broad sense, addressing the student through conversation is a consequence—albeit not one that we commonly attribute to the concept since it is not punitive.

Educators can effectively address student misbehavior in a wide array of ways. The important thing is that the misbehavior is addressed. As will be discussed later in this book, I recommend having a system of levels and progressive discipline steps to help maintain consistency and clarity, both for the educator and the students. However, certain moments and particular circumstances can afford flexible thinking and atypical action. As long as misbehavior is addressed, then there is consistency and fidelity in the disciplinary model.

Consider the fact that even courts in our justice system make deals! A criminal might enter a plea deal, receiving a lesser sentence simply because he agreed to confess something that will shorten the length of a trial. Or, a person violates a law and only receives probation. As long as they behave for the stated amount of time, then further consequences are withheld. Upon good behavior, a criminal is paroled. The President of the United States can even pardon criminals! Civil lawsuits are often settled through a negotiated settlement.

In many school expulsion hearings, students are given a second chance through an abeyance or deferral agreement. In other words, the expulsion from school is placed on hold and will never materialize as long as the student adheres to certain stipulations. The student may have *deserved* a lengthy expulsion, but instead was given a deal. Was the misbehavior addressed? Absolutely. The student had to anxiously await the expulsion hearing, had already served a corresponding suspension, and will remain on probation upon their return to school. In fact, the student will consequently be held to a higher standard because another mistake may enact the expulsion that had been placed on hold.

I am not suggesting that educators make varied discipline decisions that oscillate from one end of a spectrum to the other, or that are assigned in thoughtless ambiguity. Rather, educators should feel free to utilize thoughtful, purposeful, and strategic disciplinary methods that incorporate grace, second chances, and mitigation. Firm and consistent discipline that incorporates strategic flexibility will allow for many benefits. It will encourage students who break rules by giving them some hope to learn and grow, rather than feeling completely defeated and overwhelmed. Sometimes it's like "throwing a dog a bone." Especially with stubborn or defiant students, providing a mitigated consequence can make them feel involved. It might even make them thankful. Receiving grace is a powerful experience! Have you ever been pulled over by a police officer for speeding? Did you deserve to be pulled over? Do you deserve a ticket? If you were speeding, then yes! You broke the law. However, while the police officer slowly walked to your car window, weren't you hoping and praying that they would just say, "Okay, this time it will just be a warning; in the future, you need to watch your speed" ? Or, if you were issued a ticket, did you mail in your payment to receive a reduced amount rather than appearing in court and risking a higher cost?

Educators and schools shouldn't be afraid to make deals when doing discipline. Deals can be made while still being fair and consistent. Here are some examples of how to formalize the use of this strategy: Instead of dispensing an immediate consequence (such as a detention or suspension), draft a formal behavior contract that outlines the student's recent misconduct, the class or school policies, and the expected behaviors moving forward. Communicate the future consequences if certain behaviors result. Have the student sign it. Have a parent sign it. Formal documents like these can be very impactful for students and their families. Somehow, it makes the moment and the circumstances seem very serious. Sometimes, it makes the discipline process seem formal and binding. I've had some very difficult students completely change their behavior after they have signed a very official-looking behavior agreement. Many schools and jurisdictions mail official warning letters to families for excessive truancy. The letter is nothing more than a warning. However, the officiality of it often grabs their attention. The same is true if someone receives an official letter from a person's attorney on the law firm's letterhead.

Another alternative is an official meeting. Rather than an on-the-spot scolding, set up an official meeting at a later time. Invite the student's parent or guardian. You could invite another school member, such as an administrator or resource worker. Document the meeting, what was discussed, and the expectations moving forward.

Follow the example of the courts by creating an arrangement. It might look like this: You broke this rule and consequently deserve this consequence; however, if you do X, then you will only get Y instead of Z. For example, you had a nicotine product at school. As a result, you deserve a 6-day suspension from school. However, if you take a particular online course that provides education on the dangers of nicotine, then your suspension can be reduced to 3 days. In the classroom, if you are disruptive (and hopefully you have already described what constitutes disruptive behavior), you will receive a detention. However, if you write an apology letter and meet with the teacher to discuss it, the detention will be revoked for the first offense. By providing alternative options that are educative, and if done can reduce a formal consequence, educators and schools can begin to entice students and families to agree to many more restorative practices instead of only punitive consequences.

Should we get rid of consequences? No, that is not what I'm suggesting. A good discipline plan needs to incorporate effective consequences. However, educators can succeed with misbehaving students if they multiply their "tricks of the trade" and adopt a discipline philosophy that is more about *accountability* and less about punishment. Haberman (1995) has this to say about punishment and overused discipline:

> [Star teachers] use [consequences] only as a last resort, and recognize that punishments indicate a failure on their part, or that they may have given up on a youngster. (p. 9)

We need to make a shift from focusing on punishment to fostering accountability. Both involve consequences, but the latter is more likely to preserve the relationship, creating a platform for future growth. Can accountability be painful? Yes, often it is. It is never comfortable to be held accountable, but it is good for our growth. However, the *spirit* behind the accountability (that is, the discipline) shouldn't be to punish. It should be to *teach* the recipient so that they have a better understanding of boundaries and is better situated to change their behavior when faced with the next circumstance. If an educator can accomplish this change with a conversation or a creative form of discipline, then why do we still need to punish the student? If you can get a student to agree to something they would have never otherwise agreed to— like going to drug counseling—by reducing a suspension, then why not strive for that kind of deal? They're still being held accountable, it's just that the suspension has been reduced. Why was it reduced? It was reduced because they agreed to go to counseling. In a situation like this, you have accomplished accountability *and* an opportunity for growth. You've upheld discipline, while creating buy-in and agreement from the student. It is possible to be firm and creative!

MISCONCEPTION 7: THAT TEACHER DOESN'T LIKE KIDS

Of course, no teacher would ever acknowledge that he is "that" unlikeable teacher. Most unlikeable teachers don't even realize they are unlikeable. Truth be told, some teachers are, in fact, unlikeable. Consequently, these unlikeable teachers are going to have a very hard time winning with their students. No matter how skilled they are in most areas of classroom management, they will struggle with student discipline. And, if they don't struggle, odds are that their students behave out of a fear that breeds resentment or, perhaps to a lesser degree, disfavor. Students don't learn from someone they don't like—or at least they don't learn to their fullest potential.

Please understand that in no way am I trying to cast all unlikeable individuals into one mold. Nor am I suggesting that a person who is unlikeable to most is unlikeable to everyone. We find some teachers who are disliked by most students, but adored by some. I'd argue that almost every teacher has at least one student, usually more, who dislike them. As it is said, "You can't win them all!" However, I am referring to the teachers who are disliked by most of their students. A retort might be, "Hey! It's not about being liked; it's about being respected." Well, in the context that I am writing about, being liked means you are respected. I'm not referring to the kind of "likeable" teacher who in her unprofessionalism tries to be "buddies" with her students. I'm referring to the likeable teachers whom students absolutely love. They are the teachers whom students enjoy being with; the teachers whom students feel safe around. I'm referring to the likeable teachers who receive behind-the-scenes comments from students such as, "Yeah, that teacher is good; I like her." A student might even say, "She's not my favorite teacher, but she does a good job." That is still what I would refer to as a "likeable teacher." Within this context, being *liked* is being *respected*. The way I am using these words, you can't be respected if you are not liked.

Someone might also argue, "Students don't like me, but in my class, they *learn*." That could be true to an extent, but usually it's not. Again, students tend not to learn from teachers they don't like. I believe it has to do with human emotions of trust and a natural need to feel safe. If a student doesn't feel safe—if they feel uneasy or on edge—then I don't think they can learn to their fullest potential. True learning—that is deep and richly understood by the learner—requires a safe environment. Feeling safe and being able to learn go hand in hand.

These teachers' colleagues see that they are unlikeable. In fact, behind these teachers' backs, it is likely that many students, parents, and other educators often comment, "That teacher doesn't like kids." The line of logic continues, "If he doesn't like kids, then why is he in this career? Why is he a teacher?" Of course, there might be a teacher who doesn't like kids. However, I really do believe that almost every teacher does, deep down within the heart, care about students. Some teachers might have drifted from their original devotion to students because of many years or episodes of frustration in the profession. Some teachers might have become grumpier throughout their tenure. Even because of personal issues at home, some teachers might have forgotten why they decided to become an educator in the first place. But, I honestly don't believe that they dislike students.

If this is a misconception, then why are these teachers so unlikeable? Certainly, we'd have to accurately understand the many factors, life circumstances, and psychologies that contribute to how a person becomes, generally speaking, unlikeable. However, I'd like to provide a few factors that I have observed throughout my career pertaining to being unlikeable in the classroom. I must also mention that I have at different times and for different students been that unlikeable teacher. Fortunately, however, I was able to learn through my mistakes. I've experienced and *embraced* humbling moments where I was faced with my errors, and recognized how my actions had been perceived and in what areas I needed to make a change. My hope is that an educator who is reading this might lower their guard and consider whether or not they are unlikeable to their students. That through their authentic reflection, they might acknowledge this hard truth. And *because* they like kids, my hope is that they might alter how they come across to their students.

Here are a few simple factors that seem to create an unlikeable teacher. Said more directly, "You might be unlikeable because of one or several of these reasons." The good news is, if you can identify and then work on the reasons, then you can fix how you are being perceived.

Being too *picky* is one of the behaviors that often describes an unlikeable teacher. I'm not suggesting a laissez-faire approach to classroom management or instruction—actually, I believe in quite the opposite. I'm referring to being overly picky about things that really don't matter and that create disproportionate annoyance for students. This relates to the "pick your battles" concept. If something really isn't a big deal, then don't make it a big deal. You can be seen as a nag if you are constantly pointing out petty things. If you give students (and people in general) some leeway, you might be surprised by how much cooperation you receive in return. This is especially true with kids! Think of the 3rd-grader who comes home exclaiming, "Mom, Ms. Jones lets us sit wherever we want on Fun Fridays!" or the 6th-grade student who comments, "Mr. Smith is cool! He doesn't care if we chew gum—as long as it stays in our mouths or is in the trash when we're done!"

At one of the high schools where I worked, we decided to allow students to wear hats and hoods. Before hats and hoods were permitted, most of the students were wearing them anyways and it became a trivial rule that required a lot of effort to enforce. Also, we surveyed our teachers and the vast majority didn't see the "no hats" policy as being of any significance. The school decided, "Who cares? It doesn't affect their learning." Students wear hats at Harvard and other universities and seem to learn just fine. Some adults might argue, "But, we need to prepare them for the real world." Well, a lot of our students will work in industries that *require* hats—think McDonald's, think about the service industry, or being a pilot or police officer. Wearing a hat in a building isn't considered rude to everyone. It might be rude to one person but completely acceptable to someone else. When my grandfather died, he was *buried* in his favorite hat! Weird? Perhaps! But, to him and my grandmother, it wasn't inappropriate. There he was in his casket wearing a nice, full suit and his Budweiser hat!

I'd also respond, "They *aren't* adults yet! Let them be kids for the few years when they are, in fact, kids." Our school began to allow students to wear hats. Most students still didn't wear them. But, the students who wanted to, did. It made some of the other conversations with students a little easier. We could say things like, "Mark, I need you to not wear that shirt because it is promoting violence." When Mark argues we can respond with, "Come on, Mark. We obviously aren't trying to be picky about the dress code. You know this. We even let you wear hats. But, that shirt, we can't allow."

Dress code seems to be an issue of debate at nearly every school, even throughout previous decades with past generations. Essentially, the *school community* needs to decide on *something*. Because dress code isn't always a matter of right and wrong, this topic often becomes one of opinion, and the spectrum of opinions are often shaped by personal or family values and even cultural or generational preferences.

I liken the enforcement of dress code by school administration to the enforcement of speeding by police. Speeding is almost impossible to eradicate. First of all, there are only a few police officers on duty within a large vicinity at a given moment in time. Also, the officers on duty are attending to an array of situations. They can't focus all of their time on speeding vehicles. Furthermore, they can't pull over *every* car. The police have to make a decision of when they are going to focus on speeding, give it their attention, and then identify and address the vehicle—one at a time—for speeding. Sometimes they give warnings and sometimes they provide a ticket. Many drivers, in the absence of a police officer, choose to speed. How can a few police officers stop an entire populace from speeding, especially when so many drivers consider a modest excess in speed to be of no significance?

Likewise, how can a few school administrators stop an entire population of young people from wearing hats or challenging the dress code, especially when so many students object to standardization of appearance? For example, just as many drivers go 5 to 10 miles over the speed limit when they don't see a police officer, so do many students wear a hat when they don't see an administrator in the hallway. After passing a police officer, many drivers speed up after they've exited their sight. Likewise, after passing a school administrator in the hallway, many students open their jackets, exposing a little bit of their shoulders or stomachs—depending on the current fashion trend that marks the era.

Yes, consistency matters, but we need to stop acting like the dress code is being completely ignored and not enforced when an educator sees a student breaking it. Similarly, when we see drivers speeding, it doesn't mean police officers aren't trying to make a "dent" in the larger goal of trying to keep the roads safe.

If you give students freedom where freedom can be given, they will appreciate it and like you more because of it. If they like you (which is also to say, they respect you), then you will have more success with them through the difficult times, as well.

Another behavior that can make a teacher unlikeable to his students is being easily *frustrated*. In other words, "Just calm down a little." Students don't want to "walk on eggshells." This is especially true if they are living in a home environment that is filled with stress and strife. Students (especially younger ones, but even high school age) are already developmentally unskilled at interpreting body language and making sense of other peoples' emotions. Therefore, when a teacher always talks in an intense tone, screams and yells, or regularly makes responsive noises like "Ugh!" students learn to be uneasy. Sometimes when students experience these behaviors from teachers, it triggers bad memories of unpleasant interactions with other people in their lives, like the father who always yells or the mother who can't ever seem to be pleased enough.

What's the solution? Be mindful of your stress. Leave it at the school's doorstep. If necessary, become a theatrical performer at school. Yes, it's not easy, but it's no different from the police officer who needs to maintain composure or the semi driver who needs to stay focused while on the road. Watch your tone. Smile more. Be patient. For the most part, your students want to please you and the other adults in their lives. Be kind with them. Your intentions might be completely pure, but your body language or tone of voice confuses the young people in your classroom, which is unwittingly making you more un-likeable than you may realize.

Although there are more factors that can make an educator un-likeable, the third one I would like to mention is the most destructive and most culpable. It is *ego*. Almost invariably, if you bring your ego to the classroom (or for an administrator, your school), you will *not* win with students. Of course, we all have an ego. But, we all need to rein it in. We need to get control of our egos. So many conflicts center on a person's ego. It is most unfortunate when the adult—and not the student—is the one with the ego problem. Educators should ask themselves, "Is this argument or situation about my need to have control?" "Why do I feel the need to win in this situation? Is it really that important?" "Could I be the one in the wrong?" "Do I feel entitled to win every battle with my students just because I am an adult and they are kids?" "Yes, I am entrusted as the authority figure, but is my perspective more valid than or superior to theirs?" "What if I were the student in this situation—how would I feel or what would I want?" We might even need to be really blunt with ourselves by asking, "Am I being a jerk?" "Am I truly being fair?"

An opposite of ego is humility. Another way to think of ego (that is, in terms of how we are using it in this context) is that of dispropor-tionate importance. It is to say, "My perspective is more important than yours." Often, we are really implying, "*I* am more important than *you* are!" What a lie. What a disproportionate perspective. How damaging can it be to have an ego problem? What is the result? It makes us un-likeable! Most terribly, having an ego problem prevents us from seeing our own flaws. It shields us from the truth, hindering our ability to reflect and become better individuals. All of us need to get control of our egos, especially when working with students.

Martin Haberman (1995) wrote a terrific book, entitled *Star Teachers of Children in Poverty,* based on his many interviews with teachers. At the end of his book, he lists certain characteristics of star teachers:

- They tend to be nonjudgmental. As they interact with children and adults in schools, their first thought is not to decide the goodness or badness of things but to understand events and communications.
- They are not moralistic. They don't believe that preaching is teaching.
- They are not easily shocked even by horrific events. They tend to ask themselves, "What can I do about this?" and if they think they can help, they do; otherwise, they get on with their work and their lives.
- They not only listen, they hear. They not only hear, they seek to understand. They regard listening to children, parents, or anyone involved in the school community as a potential source of useful information.
- They recognize they have feelings of hate, prejudice, and bias, and they strive to overcome them.
- They do not see themselves as saviors who have come to save their schools. They don't really expect their schools to change much.
- They do not see themselves as being alone. They network.
- They see themselves as "winning" even though they know their total influence on their students is much less than that of the total society, neighborhood, and gang.
- They enjoy their interactions with children and youth so much they are willing to put up with irrational demands of the school system.
- They think their primary impact on their students is that they've made them more humane and less frustrated, or raised their self-esteem.
- They derive all types of satisfactions and meet all kinds of needs by teaching children or youth in poverty. The one exception is power. They meet no power needs whatsoever by functioning as teachers. (Haberman, 1995, pp. 93–94)

In summary, the characteristics are being patient, nonjudgmental, nonpresumptuous, optimistic, and genuinely interested in the welfare of students' growth. In other words, they replace ego with humility, remain grounded in reality, and are wholly devoted to their students.

MISCONCEPTION 8: THE STUDENT TOLD ME YOU SAID . . .

Working as a school administrator, a frustration of mine has been when teachers believe the things students say about their discipline meetings with me. It's not that I am mad at the teacher. Rather, I have found it to be unfortunate that the student can so easily create a wedge between two well-intentioned adults. It goes like this: I meet with a student to discuss their behavior in a teacher's class. I am stern with the student, use no uncertain language, and set clear expectations for the student moving forward. The student might have even received formal school discipline. Yet, the next time the student is around the teacher, they make a point to comment out loud for the teacher to hear, whether speaking to no one in particular or to a peer: "Yeah, the principal didn't even get me in trouble!" He might say that even if they *did* get in trouble. Or they might say something like, "The principal gave me a detention, but I'm not even going to serve it." Comments like that make some teachers feel like the discipline didn't do its job—it didn't change the student. Sometimes the student will even flat-out lie, saying, "He said Ms. Arnold's rules are stupid, but I have to follow them." I've known situations when a student is sent out of class to my office for misbehavior and the student tries to save face by saying to the teacher, "I don't care! I'm not even going to get in trouble! The principal likes me." Well, I do like them. I like all students, even though some are easier to like than others! But, liking the student has nothing to do with whether or not the student is going to get in trouble.

Why do students make these comments when they're about to get in trouble or after being reprimanded? It's simple! It's not only developmentally normal; it's a typical human response. The student wants to save face in front of their peers. No one likes to be called out or embarrassed in front of others. If the student has created their identity around being "the bad kid," then they will work even harder to create the image that they are unscathed by the discipline. Not only so, but the student might want to "get under the teacher's skin" by making these kinds of comments. They don't have much leverage in the teacher-to-student relationship, so they will use what they do have by making these cutting comments.

Unfortunately, many teachers believe the comments. They let the comments "get under their skin." How do I know? Because in many cases, the teachers tell me. You might find this hard to believe, but while writing this very section during a short break in my day, a teacher called my office regarding this very issue! I had recently spoken to one of his students. The teacher asked me to come talk to the student in the hallway outside his classroom. The student changed his behavior and returned to the classroom. He behaved for the remainder of the class. But, once the bell rang to change periods, while walking out of the classroom he said to a friend, "The principal said that isn't even the school rule—it's *his* (the teacher's) rule," implying that the principal thinks the teacher's rules are stupid. The teacher took it as such. The comment got under his skin. The teacher called my office to discuss the situation. At the end of our conversation, the teacher said, "Do you know what the student said when walking out of my class?" Thankfully, the teacher raised this topic in our conversation so I was able to clarify and set the record straight. Did it still create mistrust between me and the teacher? I'm not sure. It could have. I hope it didn't, but these kinds of student comments can disrupt trust between teachers and administrators. These comments definitely can create a wedge between teachers and administrators if a teacher takes offense to the student's comment, believes it to be true, and never talks to the administrator about it. How often does this happen?

So, what are these students doing? I refer to this wedge-creating, developmentally common, yet nonetheless entirely unacceptable strategy as the student "blowing smoke." *Blowing smoke* is a phrase to describe when a person "speaks in a certain way that is intended to make someone confused or prevent them from getting an accurate idea of a situation" (*Macmillan Dictionary*, n.d.). That's exactly what the student is trying to do. Why? Again, to save face in front of their peers and/or to "get back" at the teacher by "getting under the teacher's skin." Why do so many teachers fall victim to this tactic? I'm not completely sure, but I think it may have something to do with how personal the relationship inevitably is between a teacher and her students—which is a good thing! I think it is so easy for the teacher to take offense because the student's behavior and attitude toward the teacher and the classroom is so frequent and so purposeful. The teacher spends every weekday with their students. The teacher labors and the students labor. The teacher works hard to have them learn and to behave and to become better individuals. And then, bam! The student misbehaves and makes the teacher feel ineffective or devalued. Furthermore, the student's "smoke blowing" intensifies the teacher's hurt or frustrated feelings by entangling the principal in the situation, pinning the principal, likewise, against the teacher.

Some teachers see through the "smoke," but honestly, I think many fall victim to it. These kids are clever, right? They've been pushing our buttons since birth, when they could stir us out of bed in the middle of the night with a baby's cry. As children develop, they often use all kinds of strategies, even unknowingly, to gain their desired wants and needs. This "smoke-blowing" strategy can really disrupt a teacher's trust in their principal. And if it doesn't disrupt their relationship with the principal, it can certainly cast doubt, which is destructive enough.

Educators need to recognize the misconception produced by "smoke-blowing." Educators need to be aware of this common, kid-favorite strategy. School principals need to remind teachers that the students are *going* to try to "blow smoke." For many kids, it's natural; it's what they do. Expect it. See through it. Also, school principals need to continually foster open dialogue with teachers. Teachers need to feel comfortable conversing with their principals. There needs to be a culture where people "go directly to the source" when wondering about something. They need to ask the principal, "This student told me you said X, Y, and Z. Is that true?" They need to mention, "That student made this comment." A culture of open and effective communication helps to clarify misunderstandings and allows people to "see through the smoke" that is meant to hurt and confuse, resulting in distrust. Administrators must create this kind of culture.

MISCONCEPTION 9: IF YOU GIVE IN, YOU LOSE CREDIBILITY

"If you give in, you lose credibility." This isn't necessarily true. If you *always* give in, then yes, you probably will lose credibility. However, it's possible to ignore some things if in the end the positive outweighs the negative and if doing so isn't a matter of ethics. For example, wise parents often ignore the eye rolling of a teenager or the fits a toddler throws. When referring to his experience with fatherhood, Bill Murray, famous for being a comedian, has some incredibly sophisticated takes on the subject:

> If you bite on everything they throw at you, they will grind you down. You have to ignore a certain amount of stuff.

Most people agree with the need to pick your battles. However, we all need to make the practice of it a priority!

It's also possible to give students a second chance or a warning. Again, if you *never* follow through or *seldom* follow through, yes, you probably will lose credibility. But sometimes cutting someone a break can create an opportunity for you to *win* the student over from that point forward. I refer to this as having the student "wrapped around your finger"—that is, in a good way. Here's an example. Today, a student was disrespectful toward me and refused to follow my simple request in the lunchroom. This disrespect was witnessed by a lot of students in the surrounding area. I stayed calm and tried working through the situation with them, but they were committed to a defiant path. Finally, I asked them to come with me to my office. I started walking away and they followed behind me. Could they have stayed seated? Sure, and if they would have, I probably would have told them, "Okay, I'm going to let you sit here and then I will come get you before your next class." This approach would give them some space and would still show the other students that their behavior wasn't going to be ignored. I couldn't ignore it since it was so direct and took place in front of other students. I wouldn't want others to lose hope in the fact that the school is an orderly place.

However, my tactic worked. They did follow me. Once we got to my office, I talked to them and was able to convince them that they shouldn't have acted that way and that things are going to be so much better for them this school year if they can learn to cooperate, especially with simple requests. The student was a freshman and still maturing. In my office, they were very cooperative. As a result, I told them that I had decided that they were not going to be in trouble and that I was going to actually allow them to go back into the lunchroom, in front of the other students. I knew that they would appreciate that because it allowed them to "save face," while still showing that their behavior wasn't being ignored by the principal. By returning to the lunchroom, it created a situation where other students assumed they and I had worked things out. The student was given an opportunity to practice maturity and return to normal. They were certainly appreciative. Because I *didn't* punish them but instead worked through their misbehavior *with* them, I earned their respect. I can almost guarantee that they won't create problems for me in the future. Why? I believe it is because I *won* with them. Once you *win* with someone, you seldom have to work as hard with them in the future. It's an amazing thing.

Now, let's say they fooled me and are defiant in the future. That's fine. I'll address their behavior at that time. At that point, I can issue discipline. I didn't lose any credibility. I made an attempt to reason with a young person and attempted to win with them. If it doesn't work, it doesn't negate the importance of having tried! This mindset is no different from the famous saying: "Fool me once, shame on you; fool me twice, shame on me." Therefore, it's okay to give grace the first go-round. It might accomplish more than you would expect. And if it doesn't, you haven't lost credibility. You've only lost credibility if you let yourself believe you've lost credibility.

MISCONCEPTION 10: EVERY STUDENT CAN BE SUCCESSFUL AT SCHOOL

Every student has the potential to learn. Every student should be provided a free and appropriate public education. However, if we continue to only provide one or a few curricular paths, some students will never realize their full potential. Effective discipline practices that are relationally based and skillfully applied certainly can make a huge difference, changing the behaviors of many misbehaving students. However, some students need an entirely different curriculum! Some need an entirely different educational setting. Others need an entirely different educational focus. Alternative education must not be ignored. My belief in the value of alternative education can be communicated by a well-known quote: "Everybody is a genius. But if you judge a fish by its ability to climb a tree, it will live its whole life believing that it is stupid." I once saw a cartoon that accompanied the quote. The cartoon depicted a teacher behind his desk, making the following comment: "For a fair selection everybody has to take the same exam: Please climb that tree." Across from his desk stood a monkey, a bird, a penguin, an elephant, a fish in a fish bowl, a seal, and a dog. Behind the animals was a tree.

In many ways, this is how school is for many of our students. The academic and behavioral expectations we put on many students in our American schools are like expecting a bird to swim underwater. When the bird doesn't swim like the fish, we shame them. The bird is in the wrong setting—a place they are unfamiliar with, uninterested in, and bound to fail in. Many students need a different kind of educational setting—one that fits their interests and future.

Some students excel with traditional schooling. The current setup works for them. Other students may not excel, but still do well with it. At the other end, there are students who might do better with a different environment or curriculum, but with the proper intervention and support from adults are still within the possibility of reaching their potential in a traditional learning environment. Some students hate school but have learned to make it work for them. They don't like reading, they despise sitting all day, and they can't wait to graduate and be finished with formal schooling, but they have managed to stick it out. Some students are a little more difficult and require a great deal of extra care. They constantly misbehave and can be very challenging. However, educators can help to change their behavior with strategies and approaches found in this book.

Nonetheless, I do believe that we are providing a disservice to some students by feeding everyone the same curriculum and educational environment. Many of these "disserviced" students can pose behavioral challenges as well. Certainly this is a theory, but I postulate that for many of these students, their behavioral challenges would instantly disappear not because of new disciplinary approaches or different instructional practices but merely because of an alternative educational approach. Some students need a completely different curriculum and entirely new learning environment. I am not referring to some kind of behavioral school. I'm referring to a school setup and curriculum that fits these students' particular interests and needs. As wonderfully communicated by the quote and animal cartoon, some of these students are fish and they need to swim, not climb trees!

Let me share some anecdotes. A student who was prone to misbehavior, but had managed herself fairly well in an effort to maintain "good enough" grades, stopped me in the hallway for a casual conversation. Quite assuredly, yet respectfully, she said,

> You know what I think about school? I think we are forced to come here and study things we don't want to study. We have to learn math and English. I think we should come to school to study, but to study what we want to study—kind of like what's done at the career tech school.

Don't you sometimes love the raw authenticity we find in young people? Many times, they speak the truth!

I'm also reminded of what I've seen so often with so many students. I've seen students behave horribly at school, yet demonstrate excellent etiquette and work ethic when at their workplace. I'm referring to students with major discipline violations at school—students who have been suspended many times. I'm referring to ones who have literally cussed out principals in front of a large part of the student body. Some of these students have been allowed to use work hours (often at a fast-food restaurant) for course credit. Unlike when at school, at the workplace they are motivated. They are earning money and learning workplace skills. Whereas they might think traditional subjects in academics are meaningless, they appreciate the many requirements expected of them at work. They think showing up to school on time is stupid, but they are never late to work. They despise being told to pull their pants up around their waist when walking the school hallways, but they willingly tuck in their shirt when working the drive-through window at the local fast-food restaurant. What's the difference? The environment makes sense to them. Nothing has changed except *what* they are doing and their particular learning *environment.* Finally, they are fish in water!

Now, am I suggesting that some students forfeit their schooling, focusing only on work? Am I making a case that some students shouldn't learn Math, English, and other traditional areas of academics? Yes and no. Being someone who has earned a PhD, of course I value education. However, I think education needs to look different for different people. When I enrolled in my PhD program, it provided a curriculum I was interested in. Furthermore, for my dissertation, I was able to choose my area of research and my specific focus. I'm making a case for more individualized education for all students. But, as it relates to some misbehaving students, our best strategy might be offering them a learning experience that is more specific to their particular interests and needs. Academic subjects still need to be a part of the curriculum, but the essence of their subject matter needs to be altered. Once we offer that, I'd argue that many of these students would instantly behave, and even excel.

Am I providing all of the answers regarding the topic of alternative education and individualized learning? Certainly not! Many books are written on this topic alone. However, when discussing strategies to win with misbehaving students, I am trying to communicate the need for alternative education for some students. For some students, it is the strategy that changes behavior.

Are there school systems in America that are doing this? Yes! Is there a trend toward individualized programming? There seems to be. Nonetheless, I argue that it needs to become more of a hallmark component within our philosophical approach to public education, manifesting in effective programming changes. At what age should this start? Again, I don't intend to discuss this topic in length, but generally speaking, I would estimate that it begins somewhere in the early teenage years for some students, with a more robust entry point for a broader group of students in the early high school experience. Alternative education could be a significant difference maker for many students, creating a residual effect in reducing many behavioral issues in our schools. Expanding curricular pathways based on an individual's unique interests and strengths could unleash talents and positive behavior that otherwise remain dormant. Think about it: "When we hold a newborn, we do not see a smart or dumb kid. We see the miracle of life creating itself" (Senge et al., 2012, p. 49).

This brings me to another important topic. Behavior in and of itself is quite subjective. When creating codes of conduct and when making decisions about school expectations, which consequently impact discipline decisions, schools need to be mindful of varying cultures, norms, and expectations. So often humans make sweeping generalizations, saying "this is right and that is wrong." Dress code is a perfect example. One school might decide it is wrong to wear hats. If a student wears a hat, then the student has misbehaved. Let's remember my grandfather. He was buried wearing a hat! School leaders and teachers need to understand their students and their communities. We need to be careful that we don't impose one set of values over another set of values, especially when the essence of the matter has nothing to do with ethics. Here is a good template for making decisions about what should or shouldn't be allowed in schools: Is the behavior a crime? Is the behavior a matter of ethics, right versus wrong? Is the behavior unsafe or does it create the potential for harm? Is the behavior disrupting the *learning* environment? Most other things don't need to be converted into policy.

CHAPTER 4

Strategies

STRATEGY 1: BECOME THE FOOL AND MAKE A CONNECTION

As previously mentioned, an effective strategy for working with students is sometimes to "become the fool." Due to their current state of development and lack of life experiences, young people have a difficult time seeing situations from a broader perspective. Becoming the fool can help students to see what they can become by sharing in your own stories of folly. Intrinsically, students tend to admire educators. Other than a parent or a guardian, educators are one of the most influential forces in a child's life. Educators are perceived by students to be intelligent, hardworking, honorable, and caring. Educators are role models. Students tend to believe that their teachers have life figured out! Therefore, when a student messes up, feels stupid, has regrets, or is in the midst of making a bad choice, how powerful is it for the educator to share a personal story of triumph: a story of "rags to riches?" The educator doesn't even need to talk about how far they have come in their own life. It merely suffices that they sit before the student as a person who has achieved the status of an educator. All the educator needs to do is share a personal story of how they also were in a situation not too dissimilar from that of the student. If a student is lamenting over the negligence of their parents, an educator might have a story they can share about how their own parents failed in many ways, but how they graduated from high school and created their own life. The teacher might explain that they were determined to create a life where they raised their own children differently than they were raised. Or, when a student explains that they will never rebound from their recent mistake and suspension, an educator might be able to share a story of how they recovered from a similar mistake and consequence, becoming wiser and stronger from it. This strategy works for all kinds of students, not just in the context of misbehavior. Students need to hear that one of their teachers was considered stupid by peers when growing up, but persevered and became a prolific reader or reputable teacher. Educators can share stories about how they were once considered shy, but learned how to master social situations even if never fully comfortable in them. Becoming the fool provides students with a powerful and real story that can allow them to relate and see in the educator a glimmer of what the student can one day become. Becoming the fool for the student can provide inspiration and hope. This strategy can foster trust, authentic dialogue, and relational bonding. It can be very powerful.

Some of the best educators have developed great skill at making connections with their students. Certainly not an unknown practice, making interpersonal connections is essential for developing rapport with students. However, I have included it as a specific strategy in this book in order to emphasize the importance of making it a top priority when working with misbehaving students. By bonding *just once* with a misbehaving student, it can change the entire trajectory of the adult-to-student relationship. One moment of authentic connection can dismantle an entire history of conflict between two people. Especially with some of the more challenging students, finding a connection can take time and can seem unlikely. But with perseverance and unwavering kindness, the educator can eventually break through the student's emotional barricade to expose his vulnerability. Every human (especially a young person) wants to connect. We all want to feel wanted.

In making this strategy an intentional goal, I have been able to completely transform my relationship with some difficult students. I remember one high school female who would regularly cuss out any adult who looked at her the wrong way. As a new administrator to her school, she didn't know me from Adam (no pun intended!). She and I had yet to establish any trust with one another. In fact, our interactions began on the wrong foot because I found myself in a situation early in the year when I had to confront one of her behaviors. For weeks, she wanted nothing to do with me and she made it abundantly clear. It all changed when I was able to catch her in a moment when she and I laughed at the same thing. I don't even remember what we laughed about. But, I do remember laughing with her. In that instant we shared a common moment—a moment of genuine laughter. As we all know, laughter is good for the soul. That simple moment changed her entire attitude toward me. We connected. It wasn't completely random. I had been looking for a moment to bond with her. Perhaps I even exaggerated my laughter—I don't remember. But, if it meant seizing a moment to bond with a student who was very difficult to connect with, then a little exaggeration to win someone over was well worth it. I suppose that moment of laughter made me seem human to her. Perhaps it made me look more like a regular person than an authority figure.

Another trick I've used is finding a time when a challenging student who wants nothing to do with me is in the hallway hanging around another student whom I do get along with. Or, I find the challenging student eating lunch with a student whom I have a good relationship with. There have been many times I have purposely walked up to the student whom I get along with to make a joke, ask about their day, or congratulate them on a recent athletic accomplishment. My purpose is to have the challenging student witness the positive exchange between me and the other student. My guess is that often after I walk away, the challenging student might say something like, "I can't stand that guy!" which may receive a response from their friend along the lines of, "I like him; he's cool." This dynamic of positive peer pressure can shift the challenging student's perception of the authority figure. I'm telling you, it works!

I learned another trick many years ago from Kevin at the juvenile detention facility. He told me, "Find the one kid who is the worst kid; the one who is the ringleader. Find the kid who everyone looks up to, or who everyone is afraid of—if because of fear, people follow him. Identify who he is and then build a relationship with him. If you can win *his* trust, all of his followers will trust you too."

Another simple approach is to ask students about their own interests. Talk to them about what they care about. If they like music, talk to them about music. Let them do most of the talking. Focus on asking questions, not sharing too much of your own story. People like to do the talking. We like people who will listen to us and will laugh at our jokes. Ask students about their hobbies. Take time in class to ask about the recent football game or the latest pop culture topic.

Purposely create an inside joke or common expression with a challenging student. There was one student with whom I dribbled a basketball in the gym. It was completely random. I dribbled past them (out of sheer luck, I'm sure!) and they thought that was the coolest thing. They probably thought, "Ha, that old guy wearing a tie just crossed me over!" Afterwards they gave me some kind of elaborate secret handshake—something the kids were doing at the time. From that point forward, every time they saw me in the halls they would give me that handshake. Other kids would see us do it and because they were one of those "ringleaders," it probably helped other challenging

kids feel comfortable with me. Even at their graduation when walking off the stage, they gave me that handshake! Another challenging
student started a habit where they would always give me an awkward
wave every time they walked past me in the hall. I would reciprocate
the wave. They loved it! Perhaps they felt it was something that only
they and I had together. Perhaps it made them feel valued in a way
that other students weren't privy to. Again, other students witnessed
it and it probably improved my rapport with other students—they also
were a "ringleader."

This strategy is simple. It requires vulnerability and it breeds more
vulnerability. It creates rapport and fosters trust. I truly believe that
once you "win someone over" you pretty much have them on your
side forever more. It's the opposite of when a relational loop is broken.
If you make a strong bond, it becomes very hard to break!

STRATEGY 2: FINISH THE LOOP

The "finish the loop" strategy is one of the best concepts I have learned
about during my career. I learned about it at the beginning of my career,
during the employment training at the juvenile detention facility. The
instructor emphasized the importance of finishing the loop to every
negative encounter. To me, this idea is predicated on the assertion from
Carnegie (1936): that we as humans often hold grudges and paint in-
sults with a wide stroke of distaste for the person who offended us.
Although we may not think of ourselves as vengeful, the argument
is that once offended, it is hard for us to avoid at least some degree of
lessened affinity for anyone who hurt our feelings, made us feel stupid, or challenged us in an unwanted way. If you agree with the basic
premise of this notion, then it behooves us as educators to finish the
loop to every negative interaction.

Here's how it works. First of all, it's important to develop an emotional and social awareness of your interpersonal encounters. If you
notice you have offended someone, whether at that very moment or
later upon personal reflection, then you must make a mental note of
it. This is also the case when you rub someone the wrong way, even if
you were doing the right thing and needed to address someone's behavior, such as a manager confronting an employee for not fulfilling a
required responsibility, a friend calling out another friend on unethi-
cal behavior, or appropriately reprimanding a young person. When
harmony in a relationship is off or becomes disjointed because of an

interpersonal encounter, then "the loop" has been broken. Sometimes it can break ever so slightly. Sometimes it can be torn apart. With this strategy, first recognize that the loop has been broken, then make it a goal to find that person at a later point in time to rebalance the harmony in the relationship; that is, rebalance the relationship by retying (or finishing) the loop of the relationship.

Finishing (or retying) the loop is actually pretty easy. It requires awareness that the loop has been broken and then it takes a conscious effort to reconnect it. For example, you make a sarcastic comment and notice it offends a student. Often in this kind of broken loop, all the educator needs to do is say, "Oh, I'm sorry. I didn't mean it like that." Or, "I'm sorry, I shouldn't have said that." Another example is when you discipline a student (whether a firm reprimand, a detention, or even a suspension). Sometime later, follow up with the student. It might be a day later, a week later, or moments afterwards. Knowing when to follow up will depend on the situation and the student. But, *always* follow up; *always* finish the loop. Doing so could be as simple as finding the student later on and asking them how they are doing. Or, you could rebuild your relationship by joking around and laughing about something. You might see the student in the hall and pat them on the back or give them a high-five. If the situation that broke the loop was highly emotional and/or heated, then finishing the loop might require more of a serious conversation.

Often, just reconnecting in some way is enough to let the student know that you still care. It lets the student know the past is over and you are still committed to the student. Often, the student will pull away and try to avoid the educator because the student is still angry, hurt, or feels stupid or awkward because of what happened. Often, deep down the student just wants to know that everything's okay. If the relational loop was broken because you as the educator were at fault, then often a simple apology will reconnect the relationship. The key with this strategy is to recognize that very rarely does a broken relational loop fix itself. For every negative encounter, even the smallest of kinds, make it a point to find the other person at a later point in time to finish (or reconnect) the relationship loop. This strategy does wonders at maintaining healthy relationships, especially when dealing with confrontation and misbehavior.

This concept can also be thought of as a "relational bridge." With every relational bridge that is burned, circle back at a timely moment to rebuild it. As a servant leader, be the one to initiate this process— within an hour, after a day or week, or within seconds.

STRATEGY 3: USE VISUAL IMAGERY AND ANALOGIES

Since I'm not a visual learner, I tend to avoid it as a teaching tool. However, as an educator, I've learned the importance of accessing multiple sensory learning modes. In recent years I stumbled upon the power of using visual imagery to explain life lessons. For years, I mostly used words to talk to students about life lessons. Then, one day I found myself drawing a picture for a student and it changed my approach to many interactions. It was very simple. I drew a picture of a long line on a piece of paper. The line was probably 7 inches in length. Next, I drew a perpendicular line about a half inch into the horizontal line. I explained to the student that the perpendicular line represented the student's life at that very moment—as a teenager. The 7-inch-long line represented his entire life. I circled the part of the 7-inch line that represented his life after being a teenager. I expressed to him how big the circle was and how much life he had in front of him. I was trying to communicate to him that he has so much potential ahead of him; that he has so much life to live and can make that part of his life into *anything* he wants. Although this imagery may seem super simple, I was astonished by how wide his eyes became. Rather than hearing mere words—a lecture he's probably heard a hundred times by many adults—I could see in his body language how he really began to grasp the potential in his future. This shouldn't be surprising, because young people are developmentally prone to think in short-term representations. This visual imagery allowed him to see a concept that mere words failed to convey. Remember, a picture is worth a thousand words!

I have a picture in my office with two horizontal boxes. One is of a stick figure riding a bicycle along a completely straight line. At the end of the line is a finish line flag. The box is titled, "Your Plan." The other box is of a stick figure riding a bicycle along a line that has many peaks and valleys. Each valley has a picture of some kind of obstacle. One valley has a rickety bridge. Another valley has a small stick figure on a boat, floating on rough waters. Another valley has clouds above it with rainfall coming down. The peak after each valley has a finish line flag on it. There are several finish flags throughout the "journey." Although there are many valleys, the line of progression (which represents the journey through life) is rising along the y-axis. In other words, despite the disappointments and challenges in life (which are represented by the valleys), the "line of life" is always improving. The individual on the bicycle is growing and becoming better. It may not seem like it when they are in the valleys, but in the larger scheme of life, they are learning and becoming more accomplished. Along the way, after persevering through each valley, they find a finish line flag at the top of each peak. Ultimately, they reach the finish line flag at the end of the line. This second box is titled, "God's Plan." Whether or not the student has faith in a higher power or not, I explain that the second box represents life. The picture of these two boxes on one piece of paper is so powerful that all I have to do is simply hand the paper to a student. I'll provide a few words or sentences to explain the picture just in case they don't see the lesson in it or in case it needs to be applied to their current situation. But in most cases, all I have to do is simply hand the paper to the student and they instantly see the truth in it. Instantly, just by the power of imagery, they see more clearly, with more hope, and with more wisdom than they had before seeing the paper.

Sometimes the imagery can be communicated in words, as long as it is presented as a metaphor. One of my favorites is a metaphorical phrase, told as part of a short story. When talking to students about drama, peer conflict, or destructive behaviors, I say, "It's like this: If a stray dog or cat comes to your house and you feed it, what happens? It keeps coming back. If you stop feeding it, what happens? It goes away!" Then I say, "Often, that's how it is with drama (for example). If you continue to feed it, it keeps coming back. If you stop feeding it, it usually goes away." Then I joke, "Actually, it probably goes to someone else's house!" I've used this imagery so many times that even months after using it with a student, I can simply remind the student, "Remember the stray dog analogy?" Almost every time the student says, "Yeah, I know," while shrugging their shoulders as if meaning, "How could I have forgotten?" I've even had students say to me, "Yeah, it's like the dog thing!" In fact, there might be no other thing I've ever told students that is so often remembered by them many months afterwards—including content I've taught in class! This reveals the long-lasting impact of imagery on a person's mind and soul.

Here is another metaphorical story I often use with students. I heard this from a pastor. It goes as follows: "A man walked down a road. There was a big hole in the middle of the road. The man fell in the hole. The hole was big and it hurt when he fell in it. It took him a long time to get out of the hole. It was a horrible experience. The next day, the man walked down the same road. He fell in the same hole. Once again, it was big, it hurt, and it took him a long time to get out of the hole. On a different day, he walked down the same road. Again, he fell in the same hole! The next day, he went down a different road!" "Or," I add, "he went *around* the hole!" Instantly, the student makes the connection to the fact that they continue to walk into the same temptations or the same negative situations. They continue to surround themself with the same friends. They continue to respond in the same manner to a particular situation. They continue to talk back or to argue.

A final favorite of mine is the story of digging a hole versus building a hill. I explain that in life, each time you make a destructive or unwise choice, it's like you are digging a hole for yourself to fall into. The more poor choices you make, the deeper the hole becomes. Yes, you can get out of the hole, but it takes a lot of effort. It's not easy— the hole has become very deep! It takes a lot of work just to get back to level ground. In contrast, each time you make a positive and productive choice, it's like you are building yourself up on a hill. The more you make good choices for yourself, the bigger the hill becomes and the higher you stand. In fact, the hill can become so high that even when you make mistakes, you still are so high above level ground that the fall isn't really all that destructive. When you build yourself up on this hill, life becomes easier. It's a happy place to be. This imagery helps students see the lasting impact good and bad choices can have on their broader life.

This strategy uses the power of visual imagery to convey abstract life lessons. Stories can captivate imaginations and are one of the best tools for motivating hearts and minds. Use the examples I have provided. Without question, create your own!

As we paint metaphoric pictures for students, be mindful of what life analogies you share with them. Over the years, I've realized that students seem to struggle with relating to many of the analogies provided by adults. I've come to realize that adults often provide analogies that *adults* connect with. We need to provide analogies that connect with *young people*. We need to share *appropriate* analogies. For example, how often do educators tell students that they need to work hard in school so that one day they can get a good job? Most students, even seniors in high school, aren't thinking about their life as adults. They probably have no clue what it's like to work a full-time job. And if they do have a job as a teenager, they probably don't understand the full burden of providing for a family and making major life-impacting decisions. They don't understand paying bills, getting laid off, or taking care of children. Young people are thinking more short-term. I would argue this is why students seem to hardly pay attention when we use such examples.

Instead, provide an analogy that they can connect with. One that I've used is to discuss the benefits that come from earning money. I'll talk to high school students about having enough money as an adult to buy pizza versus always having to buy from the value menu at an inexpensive fast-food restaurant. And, I'll talk about how without a good-paying job it can become difficult to even buy fast food. Sometimes getting enough groceries can be difficult. I'll talk to them about how if you make enough money, you will have more freedom to treat yourself to something nice every once in a while (or even a lot if you have the means). I'll bring up being able to buy designer shoes or being able to take a vacation. I'll connect this conversation to the importance of obtaining an education and a diploma. I'll remind them about the benefits that typically come to people who work hard and learn how to relate well with others. I often talk about how life can be really hard or much easier; how life can be a constant uphill battle or more of a gentle glide. I'll remind them that although money doesn't guarantee happiness, it can make life a little easier. Then, I link this conversation back to their current situation, trying to focus on things like working hard in school or behaving and following the rules.

STRATEGY 4: TEACH MIND CONTROL

Anxiety and depression have become a widely recognized challenge for many youth. Educators often work with students who can be obsessive or crippled by mental fixation. Social media has exponentially compounded the gnawing force of peer pressure, image-chasing, and second-guessing one's self-worth. The brain is a powerful muscle, for better or for worse! Although I am no psychologist, I have come to realize that a lot in psychology deals with reorganizing one's thoughts. At a point in time, I started talking to students about what I call "mind control." Mind control is a type of framework. It is an approach to gain better, more healthy mastery over one's thoughts. It is effective because so many of our emotions stem from our thoughts.

Mind control begins with learning to control your mind, not situations or people. That is the basic premise. Here is an explanation: Situations happen, things happen, and people happen. Our brain reacts often with negative or primitive thoughts. If not controlled or replaced, these thoughts can cause us to feel and then act, usually in regretful and unproductive ways.

There are two useful ways to implement mind control (I'm sure there are many others!). One is to use "self-talk." Self-talk is done by telling yourself a different and more helpful narrative. Replace the initial thought, which is usually negative and impulsive, with a *truer* thought. The new thought that replaces the old one can be a rational statement that articulates a broader perspective. For example, a student thinks, "I don't have *any* friends!" Instead, the student can think or say to themselves, "I do have a good friend: Samantha." Or the student can remind themselves, "It's okay that I don't have a good friend right now in my life. I will continue to try and find one. Right now, I have a family who loves me." Also, inspirational quotes can be extremely helpful. The same student might recite the following quote: "The best way to make a friend is to be a friend" (unknown author). Another student might be struggling with wanting to fit in with his peers. He might need to continually self-talk by repeating iconic college basketball coach John Wooden's advice, "Be true to yourself." Through the years I have collected many hundreds of quotes to assist in my own self-talk. It makes a difference.

Another useful approach to mind control is to "bounce your thoughts." Habitual, impulsive, and reactionary thoughts constantly bombard our minds. Sometimes it can help to bounce the immediate thought of negativity out and replace it with a new thought. For example, a flood of depression enters your mind. Consciously stop the thought (which feels more like an emotion than a thought), and think of something that excites you. Before you know it, your entire outlook has changed. Be aware that often the negative thought (and emotional response) comes right back, even seconds after you've bounced it out and let the positive thought in. When that happens, bounce it out again. This may take several attempts, especially if the negative thought is driven by a very real circumstance or past experience. It can be helpful to couple this approach with self-talk. Understand that mind control takes effort. Your thoughts are in a battle, but by practicing mind control, you can reframe your thinking, which then adjusts your emotions. Once you get a new positive thought to stick, work hard to keep it from leaving your mind. After enough time has passed and if you continue to self-talk and bounce thoughts out by replacing them with new thoughts, you can begin to find some victory over destructive thinking.

Another component of mind control is sometimes to just be practical. This relates to the metaphorical story of the man who walked down the road and fell in the hole. Sometimes in addition to self-talk and bouncing thoughts, we need also to take actionable steps to assist our situation. Specifically related to navigating conflict with teachers or peers, here are some simple recommendations that I provide to students: Walk away from a situation (take a break); breathe; *state* your feelings instead of spewing them; make polite, reasonable requests (not demands). Each of these recommendations may apply to different scenarios, but all of them can be useful. A lot of negative thoughts and emotional frustration of young people can come from interpersonal conflict, and since young people haven't yet mastered many of the skills necessary to navigate such circumstances, these practical "go-to" coping skills can prove to be invaluable in the midst of such moments.

STRATEGY 5: GIVE PERMISSION TO EXIT

Providing students with the permission to exit a situation is one of the easiest and most effective strategies for handling and often preventing discipline situations with students. Why it is not a more regular practice, I'm not sure. Maybe it is because of supervision concerns. Perhaps it's because once we are in the midst of a power struggle, adults find it difficult to back away. Or, it might even simply be because we haven't made it a common practice. So much of society over the past 50–70 years has been based on compliance. When an authority figure used to say, "Do this or that," the subordinate person did it! However, we know that society has changed over the past decades. Now, it is common to question authority. Fraud and corruption among some in authority have taught us to not always trust leaders and follow their orders. Our society is becoming increasingly vocal and independent, in large part because of social media and the platform it provides anyone who wants to say anything. Whatever we share on social media, some kind of audience will pay attention. Dysfunction in homes is becoming common. So many of our youth lack a healthy understanding of what respect even looks like.

Regardless of the scale, exact figures, or precise origins, any educator knows that many of our youth are becoming increasingly willing to defy authority figures. Similarly, the emotional outbursts we are beginning to see from some students in classrooms and school settings are a new reality. Therefore, more than ever before, we need to adopt the strategy of giving students the permission to exit certain situations before their behaviors and emotional responses explode!

The strategy is very simple. It can be permitted for anyone in a classroom or assigned to particular students. If a student becomes frustrated to the point where his next response might be offensive, disruptive, or hostile, then he needs to know (in advance) that he has permission to exit the classroom (or lunch room, office, etc.) *before* he responds— *before* he has an outburst. This allowance can and should be planned and organized. The student should know what kind of circumstances permit an exit, how he should exit (e.g., no yelling, cursing, disrupting class), where he should go (e.g., hallway, office, counselor, resource location), for how long, and what he should do when there (e.g., coping strategies, interventions, debriefing with another adult). Educators and schools should develop a set of procedures for these exits (e.g., office notification, teacher check-in, documentation, follow-up plans). Once this allowance is put in place, it can become a very effective strategy to allow a student to "get away" for a moment to cool down, reset, reframe, debrief, and/or just breathe.

Think about it. Even in marriage, one of the best practices between two spouses is to have the habit of walking away if and when one or both become too upset. Some people can stay calm when exceedingly angry, but most can't. Most lose some emotional control in their anger, remaining fully engaged in the moment (and location) of conflict. Of course, a permanent exit where the topic is never revisited and left ignored is not recommended. But a temporary separation so one or both people can cool down and reframe before reconvening can be tremendously effective. However, it should be understood *in advance* that this kind of exit is permitted; otherwise it can make matters worse as one person thinks the other person is just walking away, when in fact they just need a short break. Also, making a statement can be helpful, like, "I am angry; I need to walk away right now."

This same approach can be used with students. In fact, I would argue that it is a healthy way to deal with angry and intense emotions. Very few people, not to mention young people, have the ability to gain instant control over their emotions. It also is not healthy to hold things in and not deal with them. It doesn't help to sit quiet and fume with anger. In contrast, lashing out verbally, yelling, or kicking or throwing things also does no good! Instead, permit students to exit when they are reaching a point of uncontrollable behavior or emotional response. Allowing them to exit may very likely avoid a major disruption or behavioral choice that could lead to school discipline and further interpersonal conflict.

At one school, we designated an entire classroom for students to go to for a cooldown or reset. The room was staffed with a full-time, licensed social worker and an adult mentor. Students received authorization from administration to use this resource. It was reserved for students who had particular needs, ranging from sensory accommodations to perpetual conflict with peers, to emotional outbursts. Often students who had been suspended or recommended for expulsion because of disruptive or dangerous outbursts were serviced through this resource. Many of these students avoided future school discipline because they were able to exit classrooms and school situations and enter this special classroom *before* losing control of their behavior. Once in the special classroom, they could "appropriately lose control" under the trained supervision and assistance of the licensed social worker. Some teachers casually referred to this room as the "recess" room instead of "reset" room, but nonetheless, these students were working through their emotional outbursts in that room and not their classroom!

Another rationale for this special classroom was articulated by one of our math teachers. He observed and wisely commented, "You know, some of our students are dealing with such trauma at home— you know, things like not sleeping at night because dad was high on drugs and fought all night with mom and the kids—and then . . . we actually expect that kid to want to do math when he gets to school?" This special room allowed students in such situations to get a chance to detox from their inner emotional turmoil for a period of time during the day when they needed it most. Who cares if they miss math class for one period, one day? Most students used the room for a few minutes, ate lunch in the room, or stopped by to check in between classes. Some students would use it for one class period during the school day. Some students only visited the room a couple times a week. Sometimes, a student was dealing with such trauma or extreme emotions that they received permission to spend the entire day in the room, and that's okay! Ultimately, after a student cools down, debriefs, and resets, the goal is to get them to return to class. For some students, if they miss 10% of their instruction, but as a result are reengaged for the other 90%, that is a huge win!

Giving students *space*, not "poking the bear," and allowing time to cool down and reset costs nothing. It is free, yet can pay enormous dividends in helping some of the most challenging students. Don't we all need a break sometimes? Don't we all need our own space sometimes? Adults know how to secure those breaks or obtain that space.

Often, we have the freedom to exit many situations. We need to provide our students with the permission to exit before a situation becomes worse.

This strategy can work even when you are trying to ascertain the truth from a student. When being questioned about misbehavior, a natural response is to lie. I'm not suggesting everyone lies, but certainly lying to avoid consequences is in our human nature. Parents endeavor to teach their children this important lesson early in life: Often, in an effort to hide the truth, we can "dig ourselves deeper into a hole"—a hole of more lies and more trouble! Many times when a student is being questioned about misbehavior, especially in the adolescent years, they become focused on telling a false narrative not only to avoid consequences from school, but to soften the consequences at home. They may know that they are going to receive consequences from school, but if they can stick to a story that conceals the actual wrongdoing "just enough," then perhaps they can raise doubts in the minds of their parents before they decide on consequences.

An effective way to approach a student who is in this mental mode, is to allow them to exit after you have presented all of the facts and after you have articulated the possible consequences. Before you allow them to exit, remind them that telling the truth, even after initially lying, usually results in a more restorative, productive scenario. Then, give them a few minutes of space. Allow them to step out into the hall or to go back to their seat in class and have a few minutes to think. If you are an administrator, allow them to step outside of your office for a few minutes. Often, the student needs to be released from the pressure of the situation, so they can think clearly. They need a moment to escape the downward cycle of "digging oneself deeper into a hole" of lies. If you continue to question them without any pause, they may "dig their heels in" deeper, putting up walls in a commitment to endless defensiveness.

One time I had a student who was being questioned about a very serious situation. If proven true, the consequences could have been an expulsion from school. After much questioning from several administrators, I sensed that they were ready to go in one of two directions. I could tell that they were seriously considering a confession. However, I feared that they might choose instead to stick to a lie no matter the cost. After explaining everything to them (which is similar to the strategy of "foretelling the future with facts" that I'll explain later) they actually asked us, "Can I use the restroom?" I don't think that they really needed to go to the bathroom. I think that they wanted to have some space away from us so they could clear their mind and decide whether or not they were going to tell the truth and accept the consequences. We allowed them to use the staff restroom in the office area. Sure enough, they came back from the restroom, sat down, and with a changed demeanor—one that was relaxed and sincere—said, "I did it." Then, we thanked them and proceeded with a calm conversation in which they revealed all the details of what they had done. In the end, they were not expelled, largely because of their decision to be honest.

STRATEGY 6: TURN THE TABLES OR ASK WHY

This is where you wish I was being literal, right? Well, of course I'm not suggesting you turn the table so that the student is facing the other way (unless that's a new strategy I've yet to discover). "Turning the tables" on a student is to remove yourself, for a moment, from the position of authority. So often, behavioral discussions between an adult and a young person become behavioral oral arguments, as if in a courtroom! Accusations are made by the adult. Facts are stated. The young person is asked to answer, to explain their actions. The young person grows accustomed to the debate, often becoming skilled at arguing every point made by the adult. In fact, adolescents in particular are developmentally likely to engage in an "I'm right, you're wrong," or "You just don't get it" manner of speaking. Arguing is their forte!

If this is true, then how can we break through the argumentative cycle that leads nowhere fast? One way is to turn the tables on the student by simply asking, "Okay, is there anything that you did that was wrong?" Said another way, you might ask, "What is it that you did that you could have done differently (or better)?" You can ask a more direct statement, such as, "I'd like for you to tell me one thing you did wrong." The young person may very likely respond, "Nothing!" That would be a typical and expected response from most students, especially adolescents. After the student's denial, be patient and continue the practice of relational discipline—establishing objective positionality and using speech control. Then, follow up with, "So, you didn't do *anything* wrong? There's *nothing* you could have done differently?" Often, you may need to ask more than one question in succession to alter the young person's distaste of reflective thinking. If they still respond, "I didn't do anything wrong," then pause. Ask yourself if a power struggle has emerged, or if the student might feel overly defensive, figuratively pushed back into a corner. This entire exchange of questioning must be within a calm, conversational context. If you are effectively practicing the components within relational discipline, then you likely have created a one-on-one environment that can handle a little "verbal tango." You've likely created an environment that has quelled excessive tension and can now foster a degree of contemplative thinking. If such an environment has been created, then you might be surprised to learn how "turning the tables" on a student can often prompt a student to admit some level of wrongdoing. Then, once a level of accountability has been accepted, you can begin to engage the conversation with the student along the lines they have admitted to. From that point, you will be more equipped to confront the *whole* situation or the *essence* of the wrongdoing. You will be more equipped to have an appropriately direct, authentic conversation.

One reason this strategy works is because it approaches conversations with a question. Something interesting happens in the brain when we are asked a question. We feel an urge, a prompting to first *think*, then *answer*. It creates an entirely different feeling from when we are *told* something. Teachers know this! Now we need to employ this strategy when having conversations with students about their behavior.

Another way to approach this strategy is to simply ask, "Why?" This approach is so simple that one would think it need not be mentioned. But I think it's an important approach to emphasize. As adults, we become so used to *telling* young people, "Do or don't do this or that." It becomes second nature. Sometimes we need to pause and simply ask the student, "Why did you do that?" Or, "Why are you doing this?" It can also be phrased, "Why won't you do what I'm asking you to do?" When we ask "why" questions with a careful tone and an authentic demeanor, it is amazing what we can learn from our students. Simply asking "why" can unlock their motivations and intentions. It can spark a conversation that can reveal the real reason why the student is misbehaving. Often, it will reveal something very concrete. It could be a misconception or a partial perspective, which can then allow for an adult-led conversation that provides the student with more explanation and clarification, helping the student see the broader perspective. Also, it can create an opportunity for the educator to help the student learn how to reflect and process circumstances with a more mature mindset. If nothing else, asking "why" helps the student feel respected and involved in their experiences.

There are countless examples of when this strategy can be used. Here are a few: A student suddenly becomes stern-faced and closed off in class. They hadn't been like this in the past, but something has happened and it seems to be directed toward you. As the teacher, you talk to the student in private or quietly so the other students can't hear. You describe the changes you have seen in the student and ask, "Why have you suddenly become so quiet in my class? Are you willing to talk to me about it?" Hopefully, this begins to "break the ice" and leads to the student telling you what they feel you did that made them upset. If you never would have asked them "why," you'd only be left to wonder.

Here is another example: A student continues to look at his phone during instruction. You expect students to have all personal technology put away during academic time unless given permission otherwise. You've addressed the student more than once about using their phone. Privately, you ask them, "Why have you been on your phone so much?" They decide to tell you that their mom is in the hospital and they are texting a family member about her current status. Or, in a different scenario, a student might admit they're playing a game on their phone, which results in you talking to them about the proper time and place for such leisure activities. In any case, don't you want to know "why" they are on their phone? Knowing the "why" might not change the circumstances or even the consequences, but it can help you to work with the student to address the *root* reason why they behaved in a certain manner. It might sound overly simple, but don't forget to ask the student "why."

STRATEGY 7: FORETELL THE FUTURE WITH FACTS

It is important to communicate all of the necessary facts when addressing a student's behavior. Students need—and have a right—to know what they are being accused of, how or why their action(s) violated previously stated rules/expectations, and what the consequences/results will be. Unfortunately, it can be difficult to share—not to mention discuss—these facts when a student is initially accused or confronted. Frequently, an accused or confronted student immediately focuses on what the consequences will be. Then, they might either come unglued with anxiety or fear, or enter into a relentless mode of defense. Often, the student is overwhelmed and can think about nothing other than how their parents will respond if and when they find out, and what that will mean for their *life* (in their mind it is their life; in reality, it may only affect the next week or perhaps the next month or so).

To combat this *normal* reaction from young people, we can foretell the future facts related to the matter. I happened to use this strategy on the very day that I wrote this particular section in this book! The School Resource Officer (SRO) brought a student to my office for using a vaping device in the restroom. The SRO said he saw a vapor cloud float above the bathroom stall. The student admitted to using the device, but refused to give it to the SRO. Knowing that this situation easily fell within the scope of a school administrator, who has more freedom to conduct searches than a police officer in many situations, the SRO left the situation for me to handle. I knew that the student could refuse a search, even if justified by our school policy. That is to say, I would never *make* the student allow a search. They could refuse and then receive consequences in violation of our school's insubordination policy, but school administration wouldn't *force* a search.

Having been in situations like this before, I decided to foretell the future with the facts. I calmly said to the student:

> I understand you have a vaping device but are refusing to hand it over to us. That's fine, but this is what's going to happen from here. I've had other students in the past refuse to hand things over. Because you are still legally a minor, I am going to call your mom. I'll explain the situation and that you are refusing to give us the device. She will probably end up coming into this office and will *make* you turn it over. She might even embarrass you in this office during that process—that's what other moms have done in these situations.

After foretelling the future with facts (that is, painting a clear picture of what is to come), I allowed there to be silence between the two of us as I prepared the suspension paperwork. After a few minutes, I calmly said, "Okay, do you want to go ahead and set the device right over here on my desk?" The student immediately pulled the vaping device out of their pocket and respectfully set it on my desk. I responded, "Thank you." Then I continued to finish the suspension paperwork.

This strategy requires you to be direct. You must be completely clear—and calm—when foretelling the future with facts. To an extent, you lay all the necessary information out on the table for the student to see.

Here's another example of foretelling the future with facts. You are about to confront a student's misbehavior, which is going to result in some pretty serious consequences. You employ the strategy by saying to the student:

I'm going to come right out here and say it. I don't want you worrying about the consequences and whether or not you are going to get in trouble. I don't want you to focus on that. I want you to focus on our conversation and how you can learn from and work through your mistakes. So, I'm going to tell you right now, here at the beginning of our conversation: You are going to get in trouble for your actions. You are going to receive (fill in the blank).

If the student becomes emotional, allow the student to work through those emotions. They might need to cry, vent, or even emotionally unload as they processes what you have told them. They might need permission to have a moment to themself. But, once they have finished their initial emotional response, they will be better situated to have a discussion about the facts *surrounding* their misbehavior and learn from it. The worry over what the consequence will be or whether or not there will even be a consequence has been set to the side. It's somewhat like ripping off a Band-Aid. In some situations, you need to go ahead and do it. Once the facts of the future have been shared, the student now has more room in their mind, so to speak, to process through what their misbehavior was, why it is problematic, and what they can learn from the experience moving forward.

Saying all of this, I want to be perfectly clear that I am not in any way suggesting that an educator should or can make a disciplinary decision *before* a student receives due process or has the opportunity to hear and share information about a particular matter. I believe in and recommend quite the opposite. So, this strategy is not in contradiction to due process or open questioning and testimony. Once facts are already obtained and both sides have had the opportunity to hear, share, and defend the necessary information, this strategy proposes that the consequence—the impending item of curiosity—be exposed so that the student isn't left wondering but can instead engage in the most important component within discipline, which is *learning* from mistakes. If the educator doesn't yet have all of the facts, they can say something like, "I still need more information and I need to hear more from you, *but if the facts are what they appear to be at this moment,* the result is likely to be (fill in the blank)." The educator can couple their statement with, "Now, I'd like for you to answer some additional questions about the (misbehavior) situation."

Foretelling the future with facts helps a student acquire and process the necessary information *before* his emotions or defense mechanisms interfere with the discipline process. This strategy helps to create the kind of one-on-one environment that makes relational discipline more effective. Foretelling the future with facts is like telling a story. Everyone enjoys a good story. Stories have a way of capturing our attention. Foretelling the future with facts helps the student see, from start to finish, what is about to happen so that they are more prepared to *think through* the upcoming conversation at the start of the discipline meeting.

STRATEGY 8: A *NEW* FIRST DAY OF SCHOOL

Harry and Rosemary Wong (2001) famously wrote about the incredible importance of beginning the school year off on the right foot. In *The First Days of School*, they assert:

> What you do on the first days of school will determine your success or failure for the rest of the school year. You will either win or lose your class on the first days of school. (p. 3)

Their ageless book is centered on this idea and it masterfully explains how teachers can make their classrooms into well-oiled machines, done with such impeccable and purposeful planning that the remainder of the school year will be a breeze. Much of their book focuses on having solid classroom routines—for both the teacher and the students. Often, I recommend or loan *The First Days of School* to new teachers or teachers who are having a difficult time with classroom management.

But, what if the first days of school have already passed? What is a teacher to do if they are struggling in the middle of the year or after the first 9 weeks? Years ago, I began referring to the Wongs' book, but with a necessary nuance. I began telling teachers that they can have a *new* first day of school! It's very simple. This is how it works. Once a teacher realizes that their classroom has gotten out of control or isn't as productive as they had hoped for, they can create a restart for *both* the students and themself. First, they will need to analyze their classroom management, ideally with the help of a principal or another teacher who has proven to be successful in this area. Then, they can reimagine and recreate their classroom environment, rules, expectations, routines, and general approach. Once their new plan has been created, they will embark on their *new* first day of school.

Although it might be the middle of the year, the teacher will need to pick a date when they will have this *new* first day. On that day, they will say to the students in no uncertain language something like the following:

Students, I need to admit something. This classroom has become too chaotic. It has become too disorderly. I am taking responsibility for it. It is my fault. I should have put in place better routines and procedures on day one. But, it's okay. Just like you, I am always learning. I have made changes to how this classroom is going to operate. Today and tomorrow we are going to learn about these new routines and procedures. I am going to explain them to you, you can ask questions, and then we will begin practicing them. Afterwards, we will spend the next 3 days practicing them. Since they are new and this is a pretty big change taking place here now in the middle of the school year, you will make mistakes, and that's okay! That's why we're going to have 3 days to practice the new changes. But, it's important for you to know, that after the 3 days, on (a certain date), you will be expected to understand and follow the new classroom setup. I appreciate your understanding and patience. These changes are going to be good for all of us in this classroom.

For this strategy to work, the teacher *must* assume fault for the classroom disorder that preceded the *new* first day of school. Also, the teacher must implement a new classroom setup with new routines and procedures. A new discipline plan will probably be part of it. Again, the teacher will likely need help from a principal or another teacher in creating the new classroom setup.

During the first 2 introductory days, the teacher should explicitly communicate the new discipline plan in terms of the expected behaviors and the progression of discipline actions. For example, "If you do this, then this will happen. If you do that, you will get this." Then, it is paramount that the teacher practice the new routines and classroom setup during the next 3–5 days. This is absolutely essential. Discipline should *not* occur during the practice phase (of course, I'm referring to discipline related to the new routines; some behaviors will always warrant discipline). During the practice phase, the dialogue might resemble the following:

(Joseph gets out of his seat without permission.) Remember, Joseph, with the new classroom rules, you need to raise your hand and receive permission to get out of your seat. (Joseph says "okay".) Now, let's practice it. Please go back to your seat and let's try it. I know this seems silly, but if we don't make it a habit, it won't happen. It needs to be a habit for you *and* me!

(Joseph returns to his seat while acting a little bit goofy—since the practice phase can feel goofy—and once seated, he raises his hand to receive permission from the teacher). Perfect! Thank you, Joseph.

It is tempting to skip the practice phase because it does feel contrived, but don't! The practice phase is essential to the success of your new classroom setup. The continual practice helps shape new habits, which are particularly important since the class has operated for many weeks under different expectations. Also, the practice models the commitment the teacher has to really begin a *new* first day of school.

After the practice phase, the classroom needs to operate according to the new plan *each and every day,* for *each and every situation.* As with any well-run classroom, your success with the new plan will only be as good as your ability to be consistent with it. Continue to reinforce your classroom routines and expectations and be consistent with your discipline approach. Maintain good relationships with your students and reap the benefits of a well-organized learning environment, even if it didn't come about until halfway through the school year.

Once teachers have established clear and purposeful routines and procedures in their classrooms, they can reinforce them throughout the school year with the use of cues. Using cues to communicate classroom procedures and expectations is really a strategy in and of itself. In fact, the cues should be taught when the routines and procedures are initially introduced. Many elementary teachers have already mastered the use of cues. For example, flipping the lights on and off to refocus the students' attention or to quiet the classroom is a well-known cue. Sometimes, teachers hold their hand up, then use their fingers to count 1, 2, 3. I know of an elementary school that uses little harmonicas to play a fun, attention-grabbing tune to grab the attention of its students. You are probably familiar with teachers who use one big clap or three consecutive claps to silence a room.

Using cues can help reinforce important habits and expectations. The cues become so familiar that heeding the command is almost second nature. The cues are easy to use, simple to understand, and require very little energy from the person providing the command.

I began losing my voice each season early in my coaching career. I asked myself, "Why am I yelling all the time to have the players come to me to receive information about the next drill or to hear an explanation of some particular skill?" I was already using a famous coaching cue: the use of a whistle! But, after blowing the whistle to stop a drill,

I would yell for my players to come closer to me or to go to a certain spot for the next drill. It dawned on me that instead of yelling, I could use a simple cue to communicate certain things to my athletes in certain situations. As a result, I taught my players and implemented the following cue: After blowing the whistle, if I raise my hand in the air, the players are to hustle over to me and "take a knee." Additionally, if instead of raising my hand in the air, I point to another coach or to a certain location, the players are to hustle to that spot and are to be ready for the next drill. The hand-raising cue was very simple to implement, the players became used to it, and I saved my vocal cords!

Although the use of cues is already commonplace in many elementary schools, I strongly recommend its practice at the secondary level. Some middle school and high school teachers have been successful using methods like the "light switch" or clapping of hands. Other teachers at these levels might feel these cues are too childish for the older students. That's fine. If this is the case, my suggestion is that these teachers simply change the *actual cue* without changing the *purpose* of the cue. For example, I once told a teacher that she could flip the lights once to communicate that group work was over and students needed to return to their seats. I worked with another teacher who decided to play music in the background of the classroom during group work, signaling that students could talk amongst themselves and move freely around the classroom, but that when the music stopped, students were to return to their seats. Another teacher decided to have a piece of paper with a different color on each side clipped to the board in the front of her room. If the paper was showing the color red, students were to remain quiet while working independently. If it was turned, showing the color green, students were permitted to talk while doing their classwork. The teacher still provided verbal directions, telling students what was expected of them during different parts of a lesson, but because she had quite a few impulsive, not-always-attentive students, she found that the colored sign helped remind students what "mode" the class was in.

I had a very simple cue when I was a classroom teacher. In my classroom, students were permitted to talk freely in class when not receiving direct instruction (as long as they were staying on task and behaving properly). However, if I stood up and began to speak, saying something like "Excuse me," followed by "Students," then students were to immediately stop talking so they could hear my next instructions. During the first days of school, I taught them this cue, we practiced it, and I reinforced it early in the school year. At the beginning, I explained the reason for the cue. The reason, I told them, was because

I wanted them to have a comfortable, casual learning environment where they could freely interact with one another. But, if I needed to speak, everyone needed to listen because what I had to say was *necessary*—that is, what I had to say was either an important directive, something to clarify or instruct their learning, or I was going to provide some kind of direct teaching. By explaining the reason for the cue, students were able to understand that it wasn't a power thing or ego move; that it wasn't about my voice being more important than theirs. Instead, the cue was needed so that I could avoid continual yelling or nagging, always having to talk over their voices. This cue worked for my classroom environment, my personality, and my students. Other teachers might find that they need more concrete cues that use noticeable sounds or provide visual reminders.

Using classroom cues to communicate and reinforce routines and procedures is a great and very simple strategy. When used properly, cues shouldn't be thought of as condescending or overly childish. They are effective for all ages, especially when one adult is working with a large group of students.

STRATEGY 9: TELL THEM WHO YOU ARE

Often, adults are perceived incorrectly by young people. It has much to do with the developmental phase the students are going through. Rather than allow students to make initial judgments about who you are and what you are going to be like, take the first step. This is particularly important during the first few days of school. Using this strategy, clearly tell the students who you are and what you will be like in class. On the first day of school, I would argue that students are focused on *only* one thing—what is this teacher going to be like? All of the students are wondering, "Are they nice or mean? Is this class going to be fun or boring? Is it going to be easy, hard, or just right? Do they get a lot of kids in trouble? Will they treat me fairly and with respect? Am I going to like them?" Rather than leave students guessing, tell them! Tell them during the first day. And as an administrator, tell a student how you operate the first time you have an encounter with them.

For whatever reason, I tend to have a serious-looking face if I'm not laughing about something. It's just my genetics! With student discipline, sometimes this works to my advantage because students aren't quite sure how to read me, which can cause them to hold back rather than act out right away. However, it also works to my detriment. In this regard, I think I can be easily misunderstood. Initially, some students might be intimidated or turned off by my demeanor. In reality, I love to laugh, I always try to stay positive, and I am unequivocally student-centered. As a result, early in my career as a teacher, I decided to begin my class each year by telling the students exactly who I am. I would share with my students the following things about me:

- I'm strict in that I expect certain things to get done. But, I'm easy-going in that I never pick battles just to pick them.
- Our primary goal is to learn. We will build relationships and have fun in the process.
- I will always seek to be positive, while never taking a bad mood out on you.
- It's nice to be liked, but I'm more concerned with doing what's right than with being liked.
- I work hard and I expect you to work hard.
- I'm interested in getting to know each of you personally and encouraging each of you to give your best in all things.
- My goal is for this to be one of the best classes you've ever had.

As a school principal, I say similar things when dealing with students for the first time. For example, if a student is belligerent or rude in the lunchroom, I'll ask to speak to them in my office—sometimes right at that moment, sometimes after lunch. I prefer to meet with students one-on-one in my office because they aren't distracted by wondering if other students are watching, since many kids feel the need to perform or "save face" in front of an audience. Once we are in my office, I might start by saying something like, "Honestly, I don't have issues when dealing with students." That statement might be an exaggeration, but I'm trying to make the point that I know how to win with students, even students who get into trouble. I might continue with, "There is no reason why you and I can't get along. That's what I like about working with high schoolers—for the most part, they are easy to get along with." Again, another exaggeration, right? But, it shows him that I care. You can make a statement like that for any age group. And, there should be truth to such a statement, or why else would you work with elementary, middle, or high school students? Sometimes, I say things like, "Kids at this school behave. They are good kids. We don't like getting kids in trouble and I hope that we don't have to get to that point with you."

Statements like these help the student to see you, as the adult, differently. You are reshaping their initial perception that adults exist to get students in trouble. Your language is explicit and positive and it paints a picture of what your true intentions are. Does this mean that you don't discipline students? Of course not. But, it helps plant a positive perception of you in the student's mind, which gives you a better platform to work from.

Sometimes we need to write down what we believe and how we want to live. The experiential act of writing something down can help us solidify our thoughts. I like this paraphrase of a John Maxwell quote: "To stay focused on something, write it down and put it before you." A good practice is to develop and adhere to a discipline motto or mantra. It can serve as a type of creed to keep you consistent in your handling of discipline situations. It can help hold you accountable. It can serve as a vision statement. This motto or mantra—this creed—is for *you*. It is for you, not the students. Although, once it is developed, you can certainly choose to share it with them.

At one point in my career as a school administrator, I created a mantra for my leadership. It was: "Always Calm, Always Sincere, Always Positive." I posted it in my office to serve as a reminder of how I wanted to behave as a leader. I've kept it in my office over the years. Sometimes I look at it as a reminder. At other moments it is an evaluation tool, encouraging me to reflect, "Am I living up to my own expectations, to my own mantra?"

I think it is helpful to create a motto or mantra for your approach to discipline. You can include it in your discipline plan if you want. Here are some possible options:

- Be Consistent, Calm, and Caring.
- Be Firm, Clear, and Consistent.
- Be Firm and Consistent, but have an "I'm for You" Attitude.
- Be Fair and Clear.
- Always Follow Through.
- Stick to the Plan.
- Remember Why You Chose This Profession.
- Be the Adult, but Understand the Kid.
- Pause, then Act.
- Manage the Classroom; Motivate the Students; Teach the Students.

- Don't Take Things Personally.
- Smile, Laugh, Have Fun.

STRATEGY 10: THE BEST STRATEGY:
NETWORK WITH WINNING TEACHERS

This strategy could be the best advice you receive in this book. Ready? Okay, here's your best resource for learning how to win with your students: Network with other teachers who are already winning with students! Obvious as it may sound, we have to honestly ask ourselves if we are taking advantage of this completely free resource.

Collaboration and networking are nothing new in the sandbox of self-improvement. However, I'd like to emphasize the merit of learning from other teachers who are already winning with students. At a point in my career, something about schools became incredibly clear to me, and this phenomenon inspired me to ask: Why is it that some students act so horribly for some teachers, yet behave perfectly for others? Think about this question for a moment. It really is a remarkable idea to ponder. Very rarely is there a student who is "bad" for all of his teachers. Usually, there is at least one teacher whom he will behave for. Often, the student is actually really good, really respectful with that one teacher. What in the world is going on? Does that teacher have a magic wand?

Sure, there are students who are defiant in all of their classes and with all of the educators in their lives; but honestly, there are *very few* students who misbehave for *every single person*. Someone, somewhere, has found a way to win with even the most challenging student. That's what this strategy is about. Let's find that one person and learn from them! Let's observe their interactions with the student. Let's hear about their strategies, their approach. Here's an idea: Let's ask *the student* why they like this one person. They'll probably tell you exactly why. The student might understand even better than the teacher the reasons why that teacher is so effective.

I stumbled upon this realization—that few students misbehave for everyone—when I was a teacher. I was talking to a handful of students in my classroom. I certainly wasn't trying to gossip about anyone, but the students just began to talk—you know how high school kids can be! They began telling me how they disliked this teacher and that teacher. They said things like, "He's a horrible teacher" and "I can't stand that teacher." Knowing that this wasn't a productive conversation to engage in, I asked, "What teachers do you like? Who are your favorite teachers?" Each of the students rattled off two or three teachers whom they absolutely loved, or who, at a minimum, they considered to be good teachers. I realized two things at that moment. First, it was super encouraging to hear that they *all* had two or three awesome teachers. But, secondly, this also meant that they had three or four who didn't make the list. In fact, they considered those teachers to be "bad." With kids, no matter the age, it seems like there are only two categories when evaluating teachers—one extreme or the other. To students, it seems a teacher is either good or bad. If there is a third category, then maybe it's reserved for the teachers who are life-changers—the best of the best! Think about it. You can ask a 6th-grade student which teachers they liked throughout all of elementary school. They'll name the ones they liked, and not mention the others. You can ask, "Well, what about Ms. Jones? Didn't you like her?" And their answer will be, "Nope—didn't like her!" This phenomenon may likely be true with all students. We may not realize it because so many students have become skilled at seeming compliant. They've learned how to behave for everyone because doing so is expected and fitting; however, it doesn't mean they *want* to behave.

I've tried to apply the truth in this phenomenon to my practice as a principal when working with teachers. A teacher will express their frustration with a particular student. They will share with me all the ways the student misbehaves. Perhaps, the teacher has sent the student to the office on several occasions and has progressed through multiple disciplinary steps in their classroom. Trying not to sound condescending, I've learned to offer the following suggestion, which is really the best resource available: "Mrs. Watson isn't having any problems with this student. Would you be willing to talk to her sometime about how she works with them and what strategies she has found to be effective?" A different sentence could be, "This student is doing well in Mrs. Watson's class. Why don't you send her an email to see if she has any ideas to share?" I've also said things like, "Ms. Jackson was really good with this student last year. It might be good for you to chat with her sometime."

At one school, we tried to make this kind of networking more a part of the school culture. At the bottom of our Behavior Level Matrix, we list the following statement for teachers:

Your best resource for behavior strategies may likely be another teacher. Very seldom is a misbehaving student displaying such behavior for ALL of his/her teachers. Find and network with the teacher(s) who has found "the secret" to classroom management for the student in question.

We started to see teachers reach out to other teachers, even through email, asking, "Is (a student) behaving in your classroom? What behaviors are you seeing? If they are doing well, can you share what is working?" Almost always, there is at least one teacher (often more) who has found "the secret" to working with the typically challenging student. Just the other week, a younger teacher wrote a long, detailed email in response to one of these teacher inquiries. The email was filled with great strategies—very specific and very individualized for that student. Of course, be careful what you write in an email. It always needs to be objective and fact-based. Ask yourself, "Would I be okay if the student's parent/guardian read this, or if my supervisor read it?" Just an aside!

Everything I am sharing in this book has come from my own journey, from my own learning. I've learned through trial and error. I've struggled through many situations, with new situations often presenting the greatest challenges. But, from each experience, I've learned more and better strategies. I've also learned an enormous amount from other people. Often, I've learned simply by observing them. Think about Kevin at the juvenile detention facility! So, I encourage you: Network with other educators who are already winning with misbehaving students!

CHAPTER 5

Resources and Conceptual Models

RESOURCE 1: MATRIX OF BEHAVIOR LEVELS

Positive Behavioral Interventions and Supports (PBIS) has popularized the use of behavior level frameworks in K–12 schools. The basic concept is that behaviors differ when it comes to the *level* of severity. Accordingly, reactions or consequences will fall along a spectrum based on the behavior level. For example, hitting another student is a more severe behavior than chewing gum in an elementary classroom. As a result, the former would fall further down—in the level of severity—than the latter on a behavior matrix. Likewise, the assault would result in a greater consequence than a student who violates a classroom food policy.

Organizing behaviors and the corresponding consequences into levels of severity, when detailing them on a matrix chart, can help schools to develop consensus on and consistency with how student behaviors are observed, judged, and treated. These matrix charts can be a great way for teachers in a particular building to calibrate a wide range of opinions on student behavior. Expectations are clearer and actions taken by the staff are more consistent.

However, as a school practitioner, I've experienced some issues with creating and using behavior level matrix charts. Most of the ones I've seen and the ones I've tried to co-create make a false assumption. They falsely assume that a given behavior can *always* be categorized by a particular level on the matrix. Most behavior level frameworks are unable to account for the large differences in severity that can occur *within* each behavior. For example, there are varying levels of severity when it comes to hitting. Is it assault every time a student fails to keep his hands to himself? We all would respond, "Of course not!" Yet, a behavior level matrix can lock such behaviors into a fixed level, regardless of how the behavior can vary in and of itself. Is a punch equal to a push? On the school security camera footage, I once witnessed a push that was significantly more violent than most of the punches I've seen throughout the years. Some pushing we refer to as "horseplay" (which is probably not the most scientific term, right?) while other shoves are borderline fights. *Borderline!* Words like this reveal the gray that can and often does exist among and even within particular behaviors.

Another example is inappropriate language. There is "not nice" language, rude language, and entirely inappropriate language. To complicate this diversity further, different individuals have different opinions on which words fall into which category. One teacher might consider "that sucks" to be fully inappropriate, while another teacher regularly uses the same phrase in front of her own students. Crap. The Lord's name in vain. "Fricken'" (which is considered by some to be an appropriate substitute when wanting to say the F-word). The list goes on and undoubtedly will continue to evolve with culture into the future.

What about talking back? There are different levels of talking back. Did the student use a curse word? Was the curse word directed at the teacher or used as colorful rhetoric while the student unabashedly gave full vent to his anger? Is there a difference? Does it even matter? Did the student call the teacher an inappropriate name? We can classify some name-calling as being discrimination, racism, or harassment. Where do certain words and particular remarks fall on a matrix chart? At which level?

As a school principal, I've been in situations where I've had to place a student's behavior on a behavior level matrix, or had to meet with a student after their teacher assigned their behavior to a certain level. Most of the time, pinpointing a behavior to a particular level has created unrealistic circumstances. In other words, the true context of the misbehavior wasn't accurately or fully represented by the matrix level. The confusion wasn't just on my end. Often, teachers' hands were also tied. A teacher might have said something like, "I listed John's behavior as a level 4, but really it was more of a 1." Or, a teacher explained, "I know their words only fall under level 2 on the school's behavior matrix, but I'm telling you—the way they said it makes it like a level 5!" These kinds of conversations happened all the time! As the school administrator, I too struggled assigning behaviors to fixed levels on the behavior matrix.

In addition, most of the behavior matrices I've seen are difficult to interpret. There are so many bubbles and text boxes and flow-chart arrows that by the time I've made any sense of it whatsoever, I'm a bit dizzy! The intentions behind the design of the conceptual frameworks are good, but the final product is a document that often creates more confusion than clarity. Behavior matrices are supposed to foster consistency among educators in a school when managing student discipline, but in my experience, most of the time they "muddy the waters."

Nonetheless, the PBIS momentum, driven from both the state and my local school district, demanded a behavior level matrix. It was considered "best practice." Often, "best practice" is a term we ascribe to *current* practices. "Best practices," as we call them, are not always *best* practices. Regardless of my frustration, I followed the edict to create a behavior level matrix. However, when creating a new matrix, I decided to tackle the dilemma I'm currently describing in this section.

I began by asking myself if there is a way to look at the *levels* differently. Are most matrices leveling the wrong thing? Based on the level of severity, what is it that we want to rank? What are we looking at? What are we focusing on? These kinds of questions allowed me to identify a different angle to focus on when categorizing behaviors. I knew the matrix needed to assign levels to student behaviors. But, *how* should we do the leveling?

I realized that instead of leveling the actual behaviors, we could focus on how the behavior *impacts the learning environment*. For me, this realization began to make so much sense! The primary purpose of schooling is student learning. Rules exist in schools to keep students safe, *so* they can learn. Rules and policies are meant to ensure order, *so* students can learn. Therefore, our behavior level matrix should not be any different. The new question became, "How is a particular behavior affecting the learning environment?" Naturally, two considerations emerge from this question. The first is, "How is the behavior affecting the learning environment for *the student who is manifesting the behavior?*" The second is, "How is the behavior affecting the learning environment for *the other individuals—whether one or a few students, the entire class, the teacher, or perhaps the entire school?*"

With these questions in mind, the behavior level matrix began to look and flow much differently than the other matrices I had encountered over the years. This new behavior matrix began to *work*. It became *usable*. The school adopted the matrix and it began to guide teachers' evaluations of student behavior. It began to inform teachers on how to respond to a wide range of student behaviors. The focus shifted from how serious is this behavior or that behavior to rather how much is the behavior negatively impacting the learning environment. This new way of conceptualizing and leveling student behavior began to generate easily identifiable solutions. Is the student behavior only impacting that student? If yes, then maybe redirect *that* student. There's no need to confront the entire class. Maybe a teacher could ignore the student since their actions aren't negatively impacting anyone else, then call *that* student's parent later in the day, or meet one-on-one with *that* student. Or, are other students in close proximity the only ones being negatively impacted? If so, can a new seating chart fix the problem? Maybe teacher proximity can help. Perhaps a teacher can alter how student groups are assigned or how they function when given freedom to collaborate. However, sometimes a student's behavior negatively affects the entire class. This type of behavior needs immediate attention. Sometimes a behavior can even impact other classrooms, the hallway, the lunchroom, large common areas, or the school at large. One example would be a student who is running through the halls, yelling while out of control. Another example could be an angry student who slams a door while leaving class. The disruption from some behaviors can lead to temporary school lockdowns or shelter-in-place protocols.

There are other student behaviors that create serious safety concerns. These would include violent threats, possessing or using drugs, having a weapon, and fighting. Others could be damaging property or inducing panic. I would classify harassment and bullying as falling on this level in the matrix—harassment that meets the federal definition and bullying as specifically defined by governing statutes or local policies.

Figure 5.1 presents a matrix that organizes behavior levels according to the impact the behavior has on *others* within the *learning environment*. For our school, this matrix was easy to understand and to use.

RESOURCE 2: CLASSROOM MANAGEMENT ESSENTIAL QUESTIONS

Here's one thing I've learned as a school principal: Some teachers have very poor classroom management, which makes them feel frustrated, even miserable. I'm referring to *some* teachers. Many teachers are classroom management pros! Most teachers have become quite good but could use some assistance to fine-tune how they establish and maintain their classrooms, or need advice from time to time with a particularly challenging student.

I've also learned that most teachers aren't comfortable with admitting their classroom management flaws. Some teachers don't even

Figure 5.1. Behavior Levels

Level	Description	Affects	Example Behaviors	Example Interventions and *Consequences**
1	Behavior is confined only to the misbehaving student	Student	Refusal to get out materials	Proximity of teacher
			Refusal to work on assignments	Redirect (verbal or nonverbal)
			Off-task, but quiet	Modify or accommodate task
			Scowling or pouting	
			Crossing arms	Parent call
			Temporary movement (not distracting others)	Provide space/cool-down time
				Approach from a new angle
			Muttering under their breath	*No formal discipline*
2	Behavior disrupts others in the student's immediate proximity	Other Students	Repeated Level 1 behavior	Proximity of teacher
			Slamming textbook closed	Redirect (verbal or nonverbal)
			Dropping book on floor	Address and restate expectations
			Kicking/slamming chair/desk/object	Modify or accommodate task
			Name calling (e.g., "Idiot")	Change seat
			Using inappropriate language (e.g., curse word, but *not* directed at a person)	Provide space/cool-down time
				Remove without office discipline
			Distractive items or actions (e.g., watching video on phone, popping gum)	*Progressive classroom discipline based on repeated nature*
			Creating or engaging in peer conflict	

(continued)

Figure 5.1. Behavior Levels (*continued*)

Level	Description	Affects	Example Behaviors	Example Interventions and Consequences*
3	Behavior disrupts nearly everyone in the class	Class	Upending desk/chair/object Distractive or disruptive movement that affects others in class Using inappropriate language that is directed at a person or is discriminatory Relentless talking or noise-making Leaving class without permission	Address and restate expectations Provide space/cool-down time *Progressive classroom discipline* *Parent contact* *Office referral (teacher discretion)* *Office removal (when necessary)*
4	Behavior disrupts other classrooms or common areas of the school	Building	Relentless throwing, hitting/kicking objects Yelling or screaming Relentless or excessive cursing Open defiance of staff requests Distractive or disruptive actions that affect broader population	Monitor situation Address and de-escalate Call secretary for an administrator *Office referral* *Office removal*
5	Behavior causes or threatens to cause physical injury to misbehaving student or others	Building	Weapon Damaging property Tobacco/alcohol/drugs Self-harm Bullying/harassment/intimidation Threats Fights/assaults	Monitor situation Address and de-escalate Call secretary for an administrator Request police (when necessary) *Office discipline/intervention*

* Your best resource for behavior strategies may likely be another teacher. Very seldom is a misbehaving student displaying such behavior for ALL of their teachers. Find and network with the teacher(s) who has found "the secret" to classroom management for the student in question.

recognize that there's a problem! It's natural for a teacher to feel offended if someone tells them that they don't know how to manage their classroom or how to get their students under control. It is especially offensive if they are a veteran teacher. But the truth is, being good with classroom management doesn't always stem from years of experience in education. Some veteran teachers have poor classroom management, while some have the best. The same is true with new teachers.

Teachers also receive very little guidance and feedback on their classroom management. Unfortunately, teaching in the classroom has become an "island job," where teachers work in isolation from one another, separated by classroom walls, and unable to observe one another because of conflicting class schedules and a full load of courses to teach. Yes, administrators evaluate teachers, but only irregularly. Also, don't the students always seem to behave a little better when the principal is in the room? Often, so does the teacher! Teachers don't get to watch other teachers teach, so it's possible to become so accustomed to your own sense of what's normal that a teacher doesn't even recognize how ineffective their practices have become, or how the students misbehave for them, but are perfectly fine in all of their other classes. I'm not suggesting any kind of hubris; rather, a kind of blindness can evolve as a classroom teacher because of the isolated nature of the job. Teachers aren't isolated from students. They are isolated from other teachers.

Additionally, many teacher preparation programs underestimate the importance of effective classroom management, which results in undertrained teachers. Why? I'm not completely sure. When I mentored student teachers, I often saw the gaps in their knowledge and practice of good classroom management. And this wasn't only because they were "green." They lacked training. None of them had had a course specifically focused on classroom management. Perhaps the topic was embedded within other courses, but it didn't seem to get enough emphasis or the level of quality necessary for its proper practice. Perhaps it is because universities tend to emphasize curriculum and pedagogy with such fervor that other practical—yet no less essential—competencies like classroom management are shoved to the side or neglected entirely. What I do know is that as an undergraduate I had a professor who was a classroom management expert. He loved the topic and taught an entire course on it. He also not only embedded it in other courses, but made his stance on the topic perfectly clear by frequently saying, "You can't be a good teacher if you can't first manage your classroom well!" He'd say,

"Once things are in order and students know what to expect and how to behave, then you can deliver good instruction." The cart (curriculum and instruction) can't go before the horse (classroom management).

Each school year, there are usually one or two teachers who desperately ask me for help with their classroom management. Sometimes their request originates from a conversation between the two of us, often when discussing one of their more challenging students. Sometimes the teacher comes to my office desperate for help. Mostly, teachers traverse forward, regardless of whether or not they need help with classroom management, and no one is any the wiser—that is, except for all of the students and the teacher because they cohabitate in classroom chaos every day!

Consequently, how can we help teachers who are struggling with classroom management? How can we help teachers who are struggling with managing students? What support can we provide for a teacher who is struggling with just one challenging student? How can we assist teachers who won't ask for help or don't even realize they need it? How do we approach teachers on this topic when it so easily offends one's sense of professionalism or one's sense of effectiveness?

A group of teachers and I searched for answers to these very questions. We formed a focus group that was tasked with improving certain elements within the school environment. First, we agreed that nothing impacts a teacher more than how they *feel* each day. We hypothesized that many teachers feel tired and frustrated because of working with challenging students or even just one difficult student. Essentially, we agreed that good classroom management is essential for good classroom instruction. Also, we agreed that *every* teacher could benefit from learning something new. We felt some teachers *needed* to learn better classroom management. However, we lamented that often those who are least likely to seek help are the ones who need it the most. We feared that the ones who don't even think they need help are the ones most others would say most definitely do!

As a result, our focus group decided to approach teachers through introspection and to approach professional development in a low-threat, nonoffensive manner. We decided to use questions to guide the effective development of quality classroom management. By using questions to communicate important classroom management concepts, practices, and considerations, teachers weren't made to feel ridiculed, incompetent, or judged. As mentioned earlier in this book, when "turning the tables" on students, questions have a way of igniting our brains. We feel a need to seek an answer. When compared to direct statements or being *told* something, questions foster a level of thinking and introspection that is far superior. Questions are less likely to offend. They are not easily twisted or rationalized. Questions allow for authentic reflection. Also, a series of questions can be great for teachers to work through together, whether in formal professional development sessions or through informal collaboration during planning periods.

We created essential questions for some of the main areas within classroom management. There was a series of questions for classroom procedures, classroom rules/expectations, classroom discipline plan, and the relationship between the classroom teacher and their students. For some teachers, their classroom management flaws are rooted in nothing other than the area of classroom procedures. They get along well with their students. They explain academic information and curricular concepts with clarity. Their rules are posted in the room. The problem is that they lack clear, consistent, and purposeful procedures. The Essential Questions document asks, "Do I spend the first 1 to 3 weeks *practicing* the procedures with the students—rehearsing, explaining, correcting, and reinforcing them?

I helped one teacher with their classroom management simply by having a procedure that *always* expected students to raise their hands before speaking—any kind of speaking during whole-group instruction. Seems obvious, right? We teach elementary-age students to raise their hands, but as students become older, sometimes we forget to keep this simple, yet essential routine. So, what did their class look like before this procedure was implemented? When responding to questions, several students would blurt out answers at the same time, making it difficult to understand all of them. A student's chair was bumped, and they loudly made a comment to the boy behind them, "Hey, watch it! Teacher, I wish I had a new seat." At various moments, several students felt the freedom to have short, rather loud, conversations with the nearest peer. A student made a joke and one or two other students responded with follow-up comments: "That was funny!"

After observing their class, at her dire request, I realized that the students weren't trying to be rude or disrespectful. I didn't feel like they were *trying* to be disruptive either. In fact, it seemed like there was good rapport between the students and the teacher. So, why was their room so chaotic? Why were they seeking advice on classroom management? What was causing them to say so many times during one class period, "Come on guys, let's go; let's be quiet please" and other pleas for order?

Well, to me it became clear. They hadn't established a set of clear, simple, yet meaningful procedures. Since they hadn't established them, they certainly hadn't practiced them with the students. After I observed the class, they asked me what my thoughts were. They asked for the solution to get their kids to behave. I told them that their students seem to like them. They seem to respect them. I said they were undoubtedly kind and caring toward the students. They provided good instruction. I told them that I thought there was *one* reason why they were experiencing such chaos in their classroom: They lacked clear, simple, yet meaningful procedures. That's it! I asked them to think about their teaching and their classroom. I asked, "What are two to four things that you *must* have in order for you to teach to your fullest potential?" "What rules *must* be followed?" If this, that, and something else are in place, and students follow them, then you will be able to teach every day, and teach well." They said, "I need them to raise their hand before speaking; I need them to ask for permission to get out of their seat; and I need them to be respectful." I responded, "Perfect, now make those three things your new procedures! Tell them to your students, post them in the classroom, practice them, and reinforce them." I told them, "Each and every time a student gets out of their seat without permission, say, 'Excuse me, remember, we have to ask for permission when needing to get out of our seats,' then have the student actually try it again to reinforce it."

Addressing and retrying simple procedures may sound patronizing or elementary, but it is essential for *all* ages. It builds routine and fosters habits. Retrying holds both you and the student accountable. It implicitly communicates, "Yes, we really are going to do these things—let's do it right now, not just next time!" It helps us not forget. It helps us to avoid becoming complacent. These aren't ethical or complicated matters. They're just procedures! They are like driving on the right side of the road, putting your dishes away when you're finished eating, saying please and thank you. But the key is, they must be done *each* and *every* time! Before you know it, students will follow your procedures without even thinking. Your classroom will be a "well-oiled machine!" This is how almost all well-run classrooms work.

Because classroom management is often neglected in teacher preparation programs, isn't always observed and properly supported by schools early in a teacher's career, and then ignored as the years pass by, many teachers who have classroom management struggles have never learned or have forgotten some of the most basic solutions. The

Classroom Management Essential Questions can be a great document to guide teachers in the right direction, regardless of where they are at in their careers. Schools can use the Essential Questions document with the entire staff or in breakout groups. Teams or departments can work through the questions together. The questions can be used to foster teacher discussion and ways to share and to collaborate. The questions can be used when an administrator works with a teacher, or when a mentor helps a new teacher. They can be used with a teacher on an improvement plan. Very simply, they can be used individually, through private reflection by any teacher. One teacher decided to go through the different areas in the document and answer how they did things in their classroom. They provided administration with their answers. It was a great snapshot of their classroom management. I assume it also was a helpful process for them to think about and solidify their own classroom management plan moving forward.

The second section of the document deals with classroom rules, although if good classroom procedures are in place, the need for rules isn't as great. The third section focuses on your discipline plan—how you are going to respond to different situations and student behaviors. The fourth part deals with one of the most important components of classroom management: *You.* It deals with you *and* your relationship with your students. Just like good procedures, healthy relationships take care of most discipline issues! This section asks questions like, "Do I greet students when they enter the room?" And, "What one or two things would my students change about how I present myself?"

A fifth and final section of the document provides a list of "Golden Concepts"—concepts like "pick your battles" and "smile, laugh, have fun," which work wonders for effective classroom managers. One idea is for teachers to pick two or three golden concepts as relational goals for the school year. These can be priorities they are going to focus on through the entire school year.

Figure 5.2 is the document that our focus group created.

RESOURCE 3: BEHAVIOR CONTRACTS

I remember seeing a funny video that mocked the formality of a clipboard. The comedic episode made the point that a person with a clipboard is always taken seriously. If a person has a clipboard, they must be doing official business! They can cut in lines, ask invasive questions, enter restricted areas. They must be recording important information

Figure 5.2. Classroom Management Essential Questions

Classroom Management Essential Questions

(1) Classroom Procedures:

Do I have very specific *classroom procedures*?

Do I take time to emphasize my classroom procedures as *the top priority* the first day or two when school starts—before teaching content?

Do I spend the first 1–3 weeks *practicing* the procedures with the students—rehearsing, explaining, correcting, and reinforcing them?

Before and when giving directions, do I ensure I have *student attention*? How can I do this?

Examples:
"In this classroom, we always raise our hand to receive permission to speak."

"During direct instruction or whole-class discussion, we always raise our hand to receive permission to speak. During group work or other activities, you can speak freely, but with an acceptable, non-disruptive volume."

"In this classroom, if we become angry or frustrated, we pause or excuse ourselves before speaking."

"Each day when you arrive to class you are to immediately (fill in the blank)."

(2) Classroom Rules (or Expectations):

Do I have a few carefully selected *classroom rules?*

There are a lot of rules I like, but what are the 2–3 that I *must* have in order to have the learning environment I want?

Are my rules easy to understand and *easy to identify* when followed and when not followed?

Examples:
"We will not be rude." "Cell phones are out of sight, not in use—unless given permission by the teacher." "Behavior must not disrupt the learning environment" (then provide *specific* examples).

(3) Classroom Discipline Plan:

Do I have a *specific plan of action* when procedures aren't followed? And when rules are broken? When this happens, my first step is this. When that happens, my first step is that.

Will my *first step* be an immediate consequence (Detention or Office Referral) or an intervention (clear warning, reminder/redirection, "time out")?

What will be my *second and third steps* in discipline: an immediate consequence (Detention or Office Referral) or an intervention ("time out," one-on-one conversation, a scheduled one-on-one follow-up, a call home, temporary or extended denial of a privilege, temporary removal from class in hallway, a form of restitution in lieu of a formal consequence if restitution is fulfilled)?

Which approaches are most effective at *changing student behavior*—consistency, clarity, communication, understanding root causes and being proactive, punishment, accountability, proper modeling of desired behavior, building relationships, networking with other staff, contacting parent(s)?

For what behaviors and what situations will I write an office referral? When will I call a parent? When will I call an office to have a student removed from class?

Do I *communicate* my discipline plan to my students? Is it clear to them? Does it deter unwanted behavior?

What *battles* am I going to fight? Which ones aren't worth fighting?

Reminder:
Students are more likely to behave when they have clear expectations, consistent follow-through, but in the context of rules that make sense to them, discipline that seems fair, and most of all, when administered by someone they like and respect.

(continued)

Figure 5.2. Classroom Management Essential Questions (*continued*)

(4) Classroom Teacher:

Do my students *respect* me? Do they like (or enjoy) me as a professional adult?

Do I *greet* students as they enter the room? Individually? With conversation, a smile, compliments? As a group once everyone is present?

What 1–2 things would my students *change* about how I present myself? What would they change about how I teach or about the learning environment I have created for them?

What are 1–3 things I could *intentionally* do to *connect* with students?

Is my class fun or interesting *to my students*? Is it one of their favorite classes? If not, why? What could I do to make them look forward to my class? Are they engaged? Are they active in their learning? Am I "the sage on the stage" or am I a facilitator of *their* learning?

Am I reminding myself of how *teenagers* see the world? Do I take things too personal? Do I stay calm, get angry, or become easily annoyed?

Am I being more *proactive or reactive* in my approach toward my students?

Am I learning from colleagues who have found consistent success with their students?

Reminder:
Ignorance is bliss, but perception is reality. As educators, we must model self-reflection and continual learning, even and especially in regard to the development of our own selves.

(5) Golden Concepts:

Pick your battles.

Avoid power struggles.

When a student is angry or frustrated, give them some space—don't push their buttons.

Be clear and consistent.

When they test your patience, be calm. When they test your expectations, be consistent and explain your reasoning.

Build relationships.

Be humble. Leave ego at the door.

With every "relational bridge" that is burned, circle back at a timely moment to rebuild it. As a servant leader, be the one to initiate this process—within an hour, after a day or week, or within seconds.

Have one-on-one conversations/meetings to "get on the same page" with students.

Hold students accountable by *addressing* the unwanted behavior—it doesn't always have to be punishment. In fact, sometimes punishment can backfire and make the behavior and relationship worse.

Consequences are not always the most effective tactic.

Be firm and consistent, but have an "I'm for you" attitude.

Fair isn't always equal. Sometimes equity is achieved through *different* treatment for *different* students in *different* circumstances.

Treat every day as a new day, a new start, a new opportunity.

Don't take things personally—teenagers will mess up. Not only is it human, but it's developmentally inevitable as they mature and learn from failure.

Listen (teenagers are already predisposed to believing adults don't listen and don't really understand). Let them share their perspective and how they feel without arguing it or having a response.

Smile, laugh, have fun. Enjoy the students. Remind yourself why you entered the profession.

Don't forget the power of grace, second chances, forgiveness, new starts, relationships, mediation, and restorative practices.

Be consistent, calm, and caring.

on the paper that is affixed to that clipboard. The comedy goes further by saying things appear even more official if the paper is laminated!

There are other examples that invoke similar perceptions. Wearing a shirt and tie. Wearing a suit. Safety indicators, such as an orange, reflective vest or a traffic cone. A memo written on official letterhead. Much of this deals with perception. These objects become symbols that invoke certain cultural responses and particular attitudes. They become cues that signal how we should react.

Understanding all of this, we can use the same phenomenon when working with students. I've found much success with creating and using behavior contracts. They can also be referred to as behavior agreements. These are different from a behavior plan or a behavior intervention plan. A behavior contract is really nothing more than an understanding between an educator and a student, but it makes the contents of the understanding *appear* to be much more important because it is "official." How so? It *appears* more official because it is a "contract," and contracts are commonly recognized as being binding and important. We grow up with the opinion that contracts are a big deal. Behavior contracts also seem particularly important because they are written as an "official" document. They contain carefully constructed language—no nonsense, very technical. Behavior contracts require a signature—from both parties! That's a big deal, right? Actually, all of these components create a context and a perception that does invoke a level of seriousness from the student. I've witnessed this almost every time I've used behavior contracts. In fact, I find it somewhat humorous that the contents in and the validity of a behavior contract are no more significant or binding than a verbal warning or vocalized set of expectations from an educator to a student, but they are taken more seriously because they seem *extra* important—they, like the clipboard, seem *really official.*

I don't use behavior contracts all of the time. Often, I use them with students who have been repetitively insubordinate or defiant. I've used behavior contracts with students who after multiple attempts have not found a way to get along with a teacher or who continue to disrupt the learning environment of a classroom. I reserve behavior contracts for more serious behaviors, which can include minor misbehaviors that have become so repetitive that they are no longer minor. Sometimes, I've used the behavior contract in place of a traditional consequence. The behavior contract *is* the consequence.

Someone might react by sarcastically saying, "Wow, I bet that will change the student's behavior—all they had to do was sign a piece of paper!" Well, for whatever reason (perhaps it's this "official" phenomenon), my experience has been that it *does* change the student's behavior. It changes the student's behavior because the contract, in no uncertain terms, spells out exactly what the problematic behavior is, what must change, and what will result if it doesn't change.

I have many stories I could share, but one in particular stands out. I remember a boy who was giving a teacher a really hard time. Typically, this teacher didn't have many discipline problems with students, but this student was a tough one and for whatever reason he was committed to making their life miserable. He never did anything major, but he continued to make little disruptions day after day. Also, he would make rude comments and just had a bad attitude in her class. He was really getting under their skin. I knew detentions or after-school consequences wouldn't change his behavior. I didn't have many recommendations for the teacher. They had good classroom management and were skilled at getting along with students. For whatever reason, he was just being difficult for them in that one class. As a side note, many times I've used behavior contracts to fix situations like the one I'm describing, when a student is continually disruptive in just one class and we are having trouble figuring out why the student is misbehaving and we don't yet know how to change their behavior. The teacher and I spoke to one another and I suggested a behavior contract. The teacher and I created one and then I met with the student. I had him sign the document. I made the meeting seem like a really big deal—it was a big deal, but I wanted to make sure it seemed *extra official*. He signed the contract, was given a copy, and I had one mailed to his parent. You probably wouldn't believe it, but not once did he cause another problem for that teacher. And this certainly was a challenging student. He was a kid who, if he wanted to, could make a lot of teachers miserable.

In terms of process, the student signs the document, is given a copy, and I recommend you send it home to the parent as well. Moving forward, everyone has a written, signed, common understanding of what is expected and what will result if expectations are not met. Sometimes, the document can be titled, "Note of Understanding." That is just another name for a behavior contract. I use that title when it is more of a directive than an agreement. However, it really doesn't matter what you call these documents. You can call them behavior contracts, behavior agreements, notes of understanding, or something else you see as being more suitable. Also, if a student refuses to sign the contract, don't worry about it. The student has every right to refuse. Simply write on the signature line, "Student refused to sign." The contents of the contract are binding either way, as long as what is written in the document doesn't violate or contradict school or legal policies.

Behavior contracts are great tools for principals to use. Additionally, there's no reason why they can't be used by teachers in the classroom. They can be a great component of a classroom discipline plan. I'd recommend that teachers utilize them as a disciplinary step that is for more serious misbehaviors or as a tool to address repeated violations. Since a behavior contract might be a new strategy for some teachers, and you don't want to put something into writing that you can't enforce, it is a good idea to have your principal review it before using it for the first time. Once it's reviewed and you've received feedback, making any necessary changes, you can move forward with confidence when instituting a new behavior contract with a student.

In summary, a behavior contract is a document that states the problematic behavior, what is expected moving forward, and what the consequences will be if expectations aren't met. With a behavior contract, it is paramount that the contents of the agreement or note are *written*—and not just written, but in *official language*, ending with a place for a *signature*. Other components can be included in behavior contracts. They can list past violations and previously attempted measures from staff. They can include previously attempted interventions and supports. They can provide future interventions and support. They can become attached to behavior intervention plans and other education documents, if and when appropriate.

Figures 5.3–5.8 show some behavior contracts I've used in the past.

RESOURCE 4: REFLECTION FORMS

Reflection forms can help students to more effectively process their thoughts. They can help students to analyze their past actions and prepare for their future behaviors. A nice benefit of using reflection forms is that they allow students to have some space. The reflection form is done on their own. While completing it, no adult is there to yell at them, lecture, judge, or "spoon-feed" them thoughts. However, an adult can work with the student after the reflection form is completed. Educators can read the reflection forms in private with no conversation afterwards—sometimes that's okay! Of course, the educator should use the information in the reflection form to guide future interactions

Figure 5.3. Note of Understanding

Note of Understanding

I, _____ met with _____

on _____ (date) concerning the following topic:

_____
_____
_____
_____
_____

I understand that further incidents of this nature may result in disciplinary actions per the Student Code of Conduct.

I recognize that this conference serves as a warning and an opportunity to change my behavior.

Student Signature _____   Date _____

Staff Member Signature _____   Date _____

Parent Contacted: _____Yes   _____No   Date _____

---

with the student. In most cases, educators will want to have a conversation with the student to discuss what the student wrote on the reflection form. The conversation can become an opportunity for the educator to *help* the student further process his behavior and to better strategize for future situations.

A colleague of mine (another school principal) shared a reflection strategy that she used when she was a classroom teacher. When a student misbehaved, warranting a detention, she would have the student serve the detention with her before school, during lunch, or after school. While serving the detention, the student would need to complete a reflection form that asked three simple questions:

(1) Why are you here (in detention)?
(2) What could you have done differently to avoid receiving this detention?
(3) If it happens again, what would be an appropriate consequence?

Figure 5.4. Note of Understanding: Behavior Contract

Note of Understanding: Behavior Contract

I, _____ met with _____

on _____ (date) concerning the following topic:

_____

_____

_____

_____

I agree to fulfill the following consequences/expectations with an understanding that failure to do so may result in further discipline:

Any violation of the Student Code of Conduct may result in discipline ranging from but not limited to a warning to suspension with a recommendation for expulsion. *I am hereby notifying you that any further incidents that are similar in nature to the current situation will likely result in disciplinary action, which may include Suspension, and if appropriate Expulsion.*

I understand that this is an official notice to change my behavior, which is disrupting the classroom, the instruction, and the mission and operation of the school. Any further incidents of this nature may result in disciplinary action, which may include Suspension, and if appropriate Expulsion.

Student Signature _____   Date _____

Staff Member Signature _____   Date _____

Parent Contacted: _____Yes   _____No   Date _____

Of course, my colleague reserved the right to disagree with the student's answer to the third question, but it created an opportunity for the student to participate in the discipline process. Similar to the "Ask Why" and "Turn the Tables" strategies in this book, this reflection form encourages the student to make a judgement about his behavior. It is surprising how many students will offer a suitable consequence, sometimes even one that is harsher than what the adult has in mind. Involving the student in this reflection also helps the student to accept responsibility for their actions. If the student's answer to the third question is acceptable, or an appropriate consequence results from a conversation between the teacher and the student, then essentially, the teacher and the student have created a mini-contract. The teacher can

Figure 5.5. Note of Understanding: Behavior Plan

Note of Understanding: Behavior Plan

Dear Mr. or Ms. _____

This letter serves as a notification to the parent/guardian of _____ that your child has, on more than one occasion, caused or contributed to classroom disruption by displaying the following behavior(s):

- Persistent arguing
- Refusal to follow teacher's directions and/or classroom expectations
- Disruptive acts that hinder an orderly and productive learning environment
- Repeated conflict with their peers

This repeated behavior is disrupting the learning environment of the classroom, the instruction, and the mission and operation of the school.

I, _____ met with your child on _____ (date) concerning their behavior in the classroom to set a clear understanding of future expectations. Although staff have tried positive approaches and a variety of methods to prevent and/or change the disruptive behavior, we now are implementing the following set of procedures for school discipline when your child displays behaviors that have resulted in the need for this *Classroom Plan:*

Student Action	School Action
1st violation in a particular class	
2nd violation in the same class, same day	
_____ amount of violations during _____ amount of weeks/months/quarters (circle option)	

Disclaimer: Any situation may result in school discipline not limited to or specified in this note of understanding, ranging from a warning to the most severe level of consequence, based on what is warranted for a given set of circumstances.

I understand this notice regarding my behavior in the classroom and the contents of this letter.

Student Signature _____   Date _____

Staff Member Signature _____   Date _____

Parent Contacted: _____Yes _____No   Date _____

---

keep it as documentation, use it to justify a future disciplinary step, and can contact the student's parent/guardian so that there are no surprises if the contract is broken. School principals could also utilize this approach.

A reflection form can also be one of your discipline steps. The form can be the actual consequence. For example, if a student misbehaves in class, having already received a warning or the result of whatever discipline level (or step) has been reached for that particular classroom, a teacher could give the student a reflection form.

Figure 5.6. Notice of Classroom Behavior

Notice of Classroom Behavior

I, _____ met with _____ on _____ (date) concerning
the following topic:

_____ (Staff Member) has addressed _____ (student)
regarding their arguing and at times refusal to follow the teacher's classroom directions on numerous
occasions this school year. The teacher/school have provided opportunities for _____
(student) to change this behavior. This repeated behavior is disrupting the learning environment of the
classroom, the instruction, and the mission and operation of the school.

Any violation of the Student Code of Conduct may result in discipline ranging from but not limited to a
warning to suspension with a recommendation for expulsion. I am hereby notifying you of the following rules
in the Student Code of Conduct:

**I understand that this is my final notice to change my behavior, which is disrupting the classroom, the
instruction, and the mission and operation of the school. Any further incidents of this nature may result
in additional disciplinary action.**

Student Signature _____   Date _____

Staff Member Signature _____   Date _____

Parent Contacted: _____Yes _____No   Date _____

The form can be given to the student right there in the middle of class. Or, the student can be asked to go into the hallway to complete the reflection form. Either way, when the student receives the form, they know that they have reached a certain level in the teacher's discipline system. The student can be required to complete the form—that can be their consequence. Someone reading this might think, "But, wait a minute! They need to be punished. Filling out a form isn't a real consequence." Well, why isn't it? If you can secure formal documentation that clearly defines the next disciplinary step, you are able to have the student write the consequence in their own handwriting, from their own mind, and you

Figure 5.7. No Contact Order

No Contact Order

I, _____ met with _____ on _____ (date) concerning a formal complaint made against me on _____ (date). I have been made aware of the complainant(s)' allegation(s). I have been given the opportunity to ask my administrator questions about the complaint, as well as the opportunity to defend and/or explain my position on the matter.

I have been informed and I understand that my interactions with the individual(s) making this complaint have become disruptive to the educational process and/or peaceful atmosphere at the school. I have been informed by the administration that I must immediately stop ALL interactions with him/her (them). I am aware of the complainant(s)' identity(s).

This (these) individual(s) will be treated as if I do not know him/her (them) and I will not interact with him/her (them) in any manner whatsoever, which includes any communication, gossip with others, staring, body language/gestures, social media, and comments or looks when walking past one another. If I happen to be near him/her (them), I will not look toward him/her (them), make any comments/noises/gestures, and will make an effort to avoid him/her (them).

I have been informed that this individual has directives to notify the school administration of any violation of this note of understanding.

This No Contact Order has been implemented as a "supportive measure" based on confirmed circumstances and/or allegations of inappropriate and/or disruptive conduct. Disregarding or refusing to comply with this No Contact Order may result in school discipline, ranging from but not limited to a warning to suspension with a recommendation for expulsion.

I understand the content and directives written in this note of understanding and that failure to follow the directives can result in discipline as listed in the Student Code of Conduct. I have been given an opportunity to ask questions about this note of understanding and to state my position regarding this matter.

Student Signature _____   Date _____

Administrator's Signature _____   Date _____

Parent Contacted: _____Yes   _____No   Date _____

---

have even fostered some reflection from the student, then why isn't that a *great* consequence? In fact, with the "contract" now "hanging over their head," what if it deters them from making poor decisions in the future? If it does, then this method has helped to change the student's misbehavior! It really isn't any different from receiving a formal, written letter of reprimand from a supervisor. A letter of reprimand may only, technically, be a piece of paper, but what it communicates, the expectations it sets, and the future action it will bring if it is violated is enough to suffice as a widely used disciplinary tactic in most organizations.

Figure 5.8. No Contact Order: Harassment

No Contact Order: Harassment

I, _____ met with _____ on _____ (date) concerning a formal complaint made against me on _____ (date). I have been made aware of the complainant(s)' allegation(s). I have been given the opportunity to ask my administrator questions about the complaint, as well as the opportunity to defend and/or explain my position on the matter.

I have been informed and I understand that my interactions with the individual(s) making this complaint have become disruptive to the educational process and/or peaceful atmosphere at the school. I have been informed by the administration that I must immediately stop ALL interactions with him/her (them). I am aware of the complainant(s)' identity(s).

This (these) individual(s) will be treated as if I do not know him/her (them) and I will not interact with him/her (them) in any manner whatsoever, which includes any communication, gossip with others, staring, body language/gestures, social media, and comments or looks when walking past one another. If I happen to be near him/her (them), I will not look toward him/her (them), make any comments/noises/gestures, and will make an effort to avoid him/her (them).

I have been informed that this individual has directives to notify the school administration of any violation of this note of understanding.

This No Contact Order has been implemented as a "supportive measure" based on confirmed circumstances and/or allegations of sexual harassment. Sexual harassment is prohibited by School Board Policy and the school's Student Code of Conduct. Disregarding or refusing to comply with this No Contact Order may result in school discipline, ranging from but not limited to a warning to suspension with a recommendation for expulsion.

I understand the content and directives written in this note of understanding and that failure to follow the directives can result in discipline as listed in the Student Code of Conduct. I have been given an opportunity to ask questions about this note of understanding and to state my position regarding this matter.

Student Signature _____   Date _____

Administrator's Signature _____   Date _____

Parent Contacted: _____ Yes   _____ No   Date _____

If a student refuses to complete a reflection form, then you have a couple of options. You can simply document that they refused to complete it, and the documentation can be used in future discussions with the student, their parent/guardian, or in planning meetings with the student. Or, instead, you can move to the next level (or step) in your discipline plan. However, students need to know in advance that refusing to complete the form will result in the next level of discipline. The next level might be a detention or a referral to the office or some other consequence you have defined in your plan.

Figure 5.9. Grade Analysis Form

Grade Analysis Form

☆ **TURN THIS FORM BACK INTO ME BY TOMORROW!!!**

Name _____ Period _____ Date _____

Your current grade in this class _____

Do you have this kind of grade in other classes? Circle: Yes   or   No

If you circled "Yes," then in how many other classes do you have this kind of grade? _____

Are you trying in this class? Circle: Yes   or   No

What grade would you like to receive in this class? _____

Are you regularly doing your homework? Circle: Yes   or   No

Are you studying for quizzes? Circle: Yes   or   No

Are you studying for tests? Circle: Yes   or   No

Are you participating in class by asking questions or seeking help from the teacher? Circle: Yes   or   No

Explain why you have this grade in this class.

What have you done to improve your grade (be specific)? If nothing, write nothing.

What can you do to improve your grade (be specific)? If you say study more, explain how, on what nights, how much time spent, using flash cards, etc. . . .

Are you committed to doing the necessary things to improve your grade? Circle: Yes   or   No

Is there anything you want me to know, or would like me to do to help you improve your grade?

I have included some example reflection forms here (see Figures 5.9 and 5.10). The first is one I actually used as a classroom teacher for academic purposes, but it still addresses some *behavioral* factors, albeit related to academic performance. I'm sharing it because it might help spark some ideas for you when making your own reflection forms, whether for academic or behavioral purposes. Here's how I

Figure 5.10. Behavior Think Sheet

Behavior Think Sheet

The goal of this form is to help you make better choices so you can have a better future!
Your success is important to us!

Student: _____   Date: _____

Disciplinary Consequence: _____

Please describe your actions that resulted in this consequence.

Leading up to or during the situation, what were you thinking or feeling?

What were you trying to accomplish? Did you get what you wanted to accomplish?

What did it cost you? What might it cost you if you were to do it again?

If this situation were to happen in the future, what could you do differently? What would be the result?

Is there anything we could do to help you be more successful in handling this type of situation?

Who do you feel you need to talk to in order to restore or resolve this situation/conflict?

What steps are you willing to take to restore or resolve this situation/conflict?

- -

Met with support personnel (e.g., Administrator, Teacher, Social Worker, Guidance Counselor, Mentor):
_____

Date: _____

---

used it: Every few weeks, I would hand this reflection form to all of my students who had a D or an F in the class and require them to complete it. When completed, I would collect and read through the forms. Their answers became great pieces of data to share in future planning meetings with the students and in discussions with their parent/guardian. I could use their answers as reminders for them in future interactions. The form helped the students to take some responsibility for their actions. Many times, their answers provided insight into what kinds of support they needed to be successful. I would meet with each student individually to discuss their answers. Sometimes I would meet with them before school, during lunch, or after school. Or I would meet with them during class for a few minutes. Great conversations resulted from the use of this reflection form. We were able to discover root causes of some behaviors, and I became better equipped to provide the students with strategies and interventions to help find more success in the future.

The second reflection form is called a "Behavior Think Sheet." It focuses specifically on student behavior. The purpose of the form is to get a student to reflect upon the entire process that preceded the discipline. It seeks to help the student discover how they were thinking and feeling, what they were trying to accomplish, if anything was gained or lost. Eventually, the form asks the student about how to restore any relationships that may have been damaged through their actions. At one school, we gave this form to every suspended student and then discussed its contents upon their return to school.

RESOURCE 5: RELATIONSHIP-TYPE SCALE

How do you measure one's ability to win with other people? How do you judge who is good at forming and maintaining relationships? Some people win with some people, but not with others. How do you tell a teacher that they are, for the most part, unlikeable? That's really what they may need to hear, but telling them that might embitter instead of persuade. I've heard it said before, "No one learns from a teacher they don't like."

When wondering about how principals can work with teachers to assess their relationships with students, I created a scale (or a spectrum). It dawned on me that individuals may, perhaps, grasp a more objective portrait of where they stand with a particular student if they are able to somehow quantify the relationship; if they are able to somehow work with a scale to measure their interactions with students. This scale is by no means scientific. It is a tool, that's it.

To start, the teacher (or administrator or any other staff member) thinks about their relationship with a particular student. After recalling and contemplating some past interactions with that student, the teacher decides how the student responded to the teacher's request or instructions. The scale provides five options for how the student did respond:

- Refusal or defiance
- Disrespect or argument
- Compliance
- Agreement
- Inspired

So, for example, the teacher might remember a situation when they asked a student to sit when the bell rang. Each day, the student needed to be reminded. When reminded, he rolled his eyes. What would you label that using the Relationship-Type Scale? It's not a horrible response from the student and it's not the most important rule, but the situation can provide a glimpse of the type of relationship that exists between the student and the teacher. I'd place the response as being disrespectful or argumentative. Again, I'm not suggesting that it is extreme disrespect. In fact, it is developmentally normal for a student to roll their eyes when confronted by an adult. However, using the choices in the scale, their response isn't one of being inspired, or in agreement, and I would argue it's not even compliance. In this situation, compliance would be characterized by all of the other students who sit without having to be asked, simply because sitting when the bell rings is an expected behavior. This particular situation makes it very hard, if not impossible, to evaluate whether or not students are in agreement or are inspired.

Let's look at another situation. A student breaks a classroom rule by having their phone out when they shouldn't. The teacher addresses the situation. In response the student says, "I'm sorry, Mr. Smith, I won't do it again." Did the student break a rule? Yes. Should the student receive a consequence? Maybe—it depends on the teacher's discipline plan, previous circumstances, and consideration of consistency. But, what was the student's response and what does it reveal about the relationship between the student and the teacher? The scale is concerned with relationships, *not necessarily* behavior. It is concerned with behavior *as it relates* to the relationship. In this situation, assuming the student is being genuine, the response reveals agreement on the scale. The student broke a rule, but when confronted showed that they are in agreement with the confrontation. Could this situation be an example of being inspired? Probably not. However, what if the student (I'm going to be a little dramatic here!) responds by sincerely saying, "Mr. Smith, I am so sorry. I am overcome with guilt and I *never* want to disappoint you again! I needed this. I'm going to be a different person now!" Now, that could be inspired. That might be a little extreme for this particular scenario, but a student could respond like that, or to that effect, in other situations.

How about a student who is glowing with respect for a teacher? The teacher is their hero. This teacher will be one of those educators who are remembered for a lifetime, as someone who truly impacted the student. This would be placed under "inspired" on the scale! On the scale, "inspired" indicates getting the student to *want* to do something. "Agreement" means being able to *persuade* the student, as if they are saying by their actions, "Okay, I agree—I'll do it." On the Relationship-Type Scale, "compliance" isn't necessarily a great label. It's not bad, but it's not worth bragging about. On this scale, compliance simply means that the students are doing what they *must*, not because they are persuaded to (agreement) or because they want to (inspired). They are simply following the rules. Their behavior reveals nothing other than that. It doesn't provide much information about their relationship with the teacher. A definition of compliance: the ability of an object to yield when a force is applied. Students follow the rules because they are told to do so. If they don't, there are consequences. This is compliance, not *relationship*. This is why I think it is appropriate for compliance to be in the middle of the 5-point scale—compliance is *neutral*.

We've already discussed disrespect/argumentative. What about refusal/defiance? Well, any interaction that falls under this label on the scale is a good indication that the relationship is not strong. However, of course there are exceptions. Remember, this scale is a tool. It's using a spectrum to make sense of complex concepts. For example, a child often defies his parents. So, do they have a bad relationship? Perhaps, but in most cases, not at all! However, within the social structure and norms of schools, if a teacher makes a request of a student and the student refuses, then there is a good chance the relationship between the two isn't strong or even existent. There can be exceptions, such as a student who is being defiant because of a disability or in response to personal trauma. Also, a teacher and a student could have *such* a strong relationship that sometimes the student treats the teacher like a parent—sometimes we reserve our meanest reactions for those who love us the most because we are most vulnerable with and trusting of them. However, in most cases, refusal from a student often reveals the absence of a strong relationship or the absence of any relationship at all. This is why it is usually ill-advised to confront a student whom you really don't know well. It can be done, and sometimes it *has* to be done, but usually it invokes a power struggle, or worse. Although students are accustomed to heeding the directives from an authority (although it appears to be less and less as our culture evolves), everyone will find more success when working with students if they can form relationships that generate an inspired response instead of refusal.

In an effort to make this scale more user-friendly, I've connected the five types of responses to a set of numbers (−2, −1, 0, +1, +2), which can also be labeled by the letters that we commonly use with grading (F, D, C, B, A). Perhaps teachers can connect more readily with the grading scale! I prefer to use the numbers −2 through +2 instead of 1 through 5 because I want the number to communicate the concept that anything below compliance is to some degree a *negative* relationship. It might not be *horrible*, but it's more negative than positive. Compliance is labeled by the number "0" because it is neutral—it is neither positive nor negative. The other responses on the scale are positive numbers. They reflect a positive relationship between the student and the teacher. Figure 5.11 shows the scale.

Figure 5.11. Relationship-Type Scale

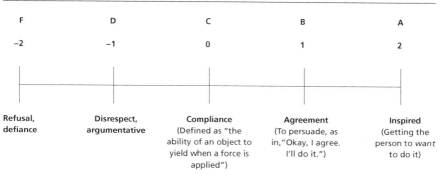

The goal is to have an "A-type relationship" with others!

RESOURCE 6: TIERED CLASSROOM MANAGEMENT PLAN

Classroom discipline plans can come in many different forms. Certainly, a classroom discipline plan needs to match the personality and style of the teacher. Also, it needs to be consistent with the school's policies and expectations. That being said, I recommend a discipline plan that utilizes some kind of system of levels (or progressive steps). However, referring back to the Matrix of Behavior Levels, not all behaviors should be treated equally. Some behaviors might fall under a different system of levels. Or, based on the severity of the behavior, some student actions might skip levels. It is important that every teacher have a system in place so they know exactly what they will do when a student does X, Y, and Z. In advance, the teacher should know what their next step will be *before* the misbehavior. If a student does this, then I will do that. If a student does that, then I will do this. Said differently, if a student makes this choice, they will receive this consequence. If a student makes that choice, the consequence will be this. It all needs to be spelled out and written down as a part of the discipline plan. The discipline plan is a part of the teacher's classroom management plan.

Also, the discipline plan needs to be explicitly communicated to the students. It would be good practice to also share it with the students' families. If you ever have to explain your actions, to a student, parent/guardian, or an administrator, you can refer to your established, written behavior plan. Elements of your plan, or even the entire plan, can be posted in your classroom. It should be in your syllabus or your beginning-of-the-year paperwork.

A major benefit of creating a specific discipline plan that has a system of levels (or steps) is that it provides the teacher with the confidence that comes from preparation. I've seen this before with teachers. By having a plan in place, specifically laid out, it can allow a teacher to feel ready for any student situation that might occur in class. When something happens, you'll know exactly what step you will take. Your plan also plans for worst-case scenarios. Planning for worst-case scenarios is very important. Even if you never end up in those scenarios, you will feel better knowing you have a plan. You will feel prepared!

When working with teachers who struggle with effectively handling student behaviors, I'm amazed at how many lack a written, well-devised classroom management plan. After working together to articulate their discipline philosophy, I have them create a multi-tiered plan for how they will handle a range of student behaviors.

The first part of the plan deals with *preventing* misbehavior. Undoubtedly, the best antidote for student misbehavior is *good teaching*! When students are engaged, given ownership and choice, and find meaningful and genuine interest in their studies, they are significantly more likely to behave. In fact, they are likely to *thrive*! Additionally, students tend to behave for teachers they *like*—teachers they *enjoy.* Relationships are key! Quality teaching and meaningful relationships *prevent* most discipline situations.

However, every classroom also needs clear and effective procedures. These procedures *are* the classroom expectations. These procedures *are* the rules. In most cases, a classroom with clear procedures is a classroom with few behavior problems. This is much of the point in the Wongs' (2001) book. When the students in a classroom are "out of control," often the solution needed is not discipline nor rigid rules. Rather, often the solution is found in implementing clear and effective procedures. For example, in *our* classroom, (1) we will raise our hand when we want to speak or ask a question; (2) we will listen to others when they speak, waiting our turn while we give them our full attention; (3) we will speak with kind, respectful language. Rather than thinking of these as classroom rules, think of them as *procedures.* This is how *we* act in *this* learning environment. Therefore, quality instruction, good relationships, and clear classroom procedures *prevent* the vast majority of student misbehavior.

The second part of the plan deals with *redirection* or *supportive action.* When students are beginning to misbehave, what does the teacher do? Strategies within this part of the classroom management plan deal with subtle, yet effective maneuvers. For example, are seating charts carefully constructed? When a student is inattentive or appears bored, how do you adjust your lesson? Do you use cues to refocus students' attention and behavior? Do you use "I statements," such as, "Kevin, *I* need for you to sit in your seat" and other statements that are clear and purposeful? Do you employ the technique of proximity? That is, do you walk toward a particular student to deter unwanted behavior. Just being near them can cause them to straighten up and regain focus. Do you move around the classroom to increase your presence and decrease unproductivity? When I was in middle school, I had a teacher who used to regularly incorporate students' names *during* instruction. For example, while talking to the entire class she would say, "Now, Adam, we are going to turn to the next chapter in the book." Or, "The second chapter, Sarah, is an intriguing portrayal of heroic literature."

I'm going to be honest. This strategy seemed strange at first. However, we became comfortable with it, and let me tell you, it kept our attention. Any minute, or so it seemed, one of our names would be spoken! These kinds of strategies deal with *redirecting* behavior, after behavior has begun to slip but far before it has become a significant disruption.

The third part of the classroom management plan deals with *discipline* or *proactive action*. When parts one and two of the plan haven't worked to curtail misbehavior, *now* what does the teacher do? Teachers need to be *ready* to have a course of action related to discipline. Typically, I ask teachers to have steps or tiers within this part of the plan. For example, when a student has crossed a particular boundary line—when they have broken a clear behavioral expectation—what will you do? What will be your *first* step? If your first step fails to change the student's behavior, what will be your *second* step? At what point will you have the student removed from the classroom? Removal is absolutely a last resort. However, every teacher needs to be ready for the worst-case scenario. With what behaviors will you immediately call for a principal? What I stress to teachers is that they shouldn't wait for these situations to happen and then make disciplinary decisions. They should know in advance what they will and won't tolerate and what they will do if that moment happens. Perhaps your first step is to restate your classroom expectations and provide the student with a warning. Maybe your second step is to move the student's seat for the class period or to request an individual conversation with the student in the hallway. At what point do you call the student's parent? At what point are classroom privileges suspended or a detention given? Whatever you decide your steps to be, you should also clearly articulate them to your students near the very beginning of the school year. If nothing else, this preparedness gives classroom teachers a sense of agency and self-efficacy.

Figure 5.12 depicts a comprehensive classroom management and discipline plan. It can be tailored to fit a reader's plan or personality, teaching philosophy, school culture, and personal preferences. However, it is worth noticing all of the separate sections within the plan. Each section emphasizes a different element of a good classroom management and discipline plan. For example, instead of having 10 to 15 rules, you can have 2 to 4 rules and a longer list of "classroom expectations." The expectations are just as important as the rules, but you might not issue discipline if and when they are ignored or violated. Instead, you might use them as continual reminders. They might be goals you are striving toward with your students. However, you might

Figure 5.12. Classroom Management and Discipline Plan

Classroom Management and Discipline Plan

My Goals:

That each student will:
1. Become better prepared to succeed on performance assessments.
2. Know, understand, and be able to analyze, interpret, and explain political and social events in U.S. History.
3. Come to appreciate the study and investigation of the world and its people.
4. Learn to love learning.
5. Learn to succeed through proper academic preparation.
6. Enjoy learning in a relaxed, yet clearly understood classroom environment.
7. Seek to be a person of character and integrity.
8. Bring the "best you" to class.

Behavioral Expectations (One Example - Option A):

- The classroom is a place for learning; therefore, in my classroom I will not let students act in any manner that disrupts student learning or my teaching—it cannot be tolerated.
- Broken rules have consequences.
- It is the student's choice to behave or misbehave, and to succeed or fail.
- On **minor** offenses, I will tell my students when they are acting inappropriately, and if they choose to continue, then they will receive a consequence.
- On **major** offenses, my students will receive a consequence without any warning.
- Class Rules/Expectations:
    1. Be on time.
    2. Be prepared.
    3. Listen and stop talking when I ask for your attention.
    4. Respect others.

Behavioral Expectations (Another Example - Option B):

- *THE BIG THREE:*
    1. Do not talk during instruction.
    2. Follow directions—the first time they are given.
    3. Act appropriately.
- Since I care about each and every student's academic success, I will not allow students to behave in any manner that disrupts student learning or my teaching.
- It is the student's choice to behave or misbehave, to succeed or fail.
- Broken rules have consequences.
- Consequences for breaking an expectation may include, but are not limited to: a warning, lunch-time detention, school detention, loss of privileges, behavioral plan, parent contact, and/or referral to office.
- All other school rules and expectations apply to students in this classroom.
- General Rule: *"Things aren't a problem, until they become a problem."*

(continued)

Figure 5.12. Classroom Management and Discipline Plan (*continued*)

Classroom Expectations:

1. Be seated and prepared for class when bell rings.
2. Bring all necessary and required materials to class.
3. Personal technology (e.g., cell phones) is not permitted if it disrupts or distracts the learning environment.
4. No profanity, disrespect, inappropriate sarcasm, or inappropriate gestures/comments.
5. Be serious about all your work—do your best the first time.
6. Seek help from teacher—you know best if and when you need help.
7. Be an active participant in classroom activities and learning.
8. Use your individual and group work time effectively.
9. Absolutely no cheating.
10. Give your best effort even in the little things.

Talking in Class:

- If the teacher is in front of the class giving directions and/or teaching, then do not talk.
- If the teacher asks for your attention, then immediately stop talking and listen.
- If you have a question, comment, or response, then raise your hand.
- When working in groups, if you have a question, first ask someone in your group; if the question cannot be answered, then raise your hand and ask the teacher.
- When working individually or in groups, often you may talk, but out of respect for other classrooms and students working within our own class, do not get too loud.

Classroom Management Plan:

1.) **Step I: Preventive Discipline:**
   - Be organized and prepared.
   - Have well-planned lessons.
   - Design lessons and activities that engage all learners.
   - Smile.
   - Affirm and encourage.
   - Be enthusiastic.

2.) **Step II: Supportive Discipline:**
   - *Silent* cues
   - Eye contact
   - Physical proximity
   - Voice projection
   - Remind and redirect

(continued)

Figure 5.12. Classroom Management and Discipline Plan (*continued*)

3.) Step III: Proactive Discipline:

(a) In a firm but nonaggressive voice, request a change of behavior.

(b) In a firmly projected voice, restate expectations and request a change of behavior.

(c) Address student behavior (take action):

    (i) <u>Inform them that you need to talk to them after class</u>. If they continue to be disruptive, ask them to move to the back of the classroom or to sit in the hallway outside the classroom. If the student cooperates with your request, then plan on meeting with them sometime before the period ends or after class.

    (ii) <u>If the student refuses to cooperate</u> and won't move their seat or won't go into the hallway, then provide them with two paths while you stay calm. They can either comply with your simple request, which is what you are hoping they will do (*tell them that!*) or you will have to contact the office for the student to be removed, which will result in more serious consequences.

    (iii) <u>During your one-on-one meeting</u>, issue the appropriate consequence (which could be an "official" warning that makes clear that a consequence will follow in the future *without* any future warnings, or issue a formal consequence, such as a parent call, seat change, loss of privileges, or detention).

Consequence Levels:

1.) Minor Violations (part c under Step III in your Proactive Discipline):

(a) 1st Offense: Meeting with teacher

(b) 2nd Offense: Parent call or parent call and loss of privileges

(c) 3rd Offense: Detention (you could reduce the length of the detention or revoke it if the student does something to remedy the situation, such as completes a reflection form, issues an apology, writes an apology letter, or some other kind of compensatory act)

(d) 4th Offense: Referral to office

(e) 5th Offense: Behavior plan (written by teacher or written in collaboration with school administration)

2.) Major Violations:

(a) <u>If situation is manageable</u>, immediate removal to back of classroom or hallway

(b) <u>If situation is extreme, potentially dangerous, or could lead to further issues</u>, contact office for assistance and/or removal.

(c) NOTE: With major violations, you can still start at consequence "level 'a'" or skip to a higher level. Some major violations may require more serious discipline from the school office.

---

choose to issue discipline if an expectation is violated on a regular basis. If so, you will want to be clear with the student in advance that a future violation of the expectation can result in discipline.

This plan includes the teacher's goals for the students. It also includes two examples of behavioral expectations and a list of classroom expectations. The behavioral expectations explain your philosophy and list your classroom rules. The classroom expectations are a list of attitudes or behaviors you want to see on a regular basis. The plan includes a section on "talking in class." I've included this to show how you can require certain behaviors for different *procedures* within the classroom environment. Next, the plan lists your *approach,* which is under the section entitled "Classroom Management Plan." This section delineates three different approaches to your discipline. Talented classroom managers know that one can prevent most "proactive discipline" by successfully using "preventive" and "supportive" measures. The ideal classroom is one that never needs to use "Step II" or "Step III" because all of the misbehavior is prevented by "Step I." Lastly, the plan outlines the teacher's consequence levels for both minor and major classroom violations.

I'm not suggesting that every plan *must* have all of these elements. However, thinking about and planning for all of these areas will help your classroom management be even more effective.

Figure 5.13 shows a wonderfully crafted classroom management plan from a teacher whom I worked with. They created this plan using the *Classroom Management Essential Questions* document previously mentioned in this book.

RESOURCE 7: THREE OPTIONS FOR CHANGE

I presented the following conceptual model at a staff meeting and was surprised, to be honest, by all of the positive feedback I received from teachers. I was surprised because the concept I was laying out for the teachers was actually pretty simple, but numerous teachers told me that it helped them to break down a strategy for analyzing student misbehavior in their classrooms. I am now referring to the concept of "the three options for change."

When a student is misbehaving in class, or maybe even the entire class is disruptive, you can walk yourself through a series of considerations. You can ask yourself to consider three options (or areas) for change:

(1) Change the Environment.
(2) Change the Relationship.
(3) Change the Person.

You very well may find the solution to your situation in one of these areas. Also, if you give careful and continual attention to these three areas, you should find that they provide great preventative measures to avoid discipline issues in the first place.

Figure 5.13. Example of Teacher's Classroom Management Plan

Example of Teacher's Classroom Management Plan

(1) Classroom Procedures

Daily objective and assignments are posted on front white board. Plans for the week are posted on cabinet doors.

All work is placed in bins, organized by class and date (for easy pickup when absent). All work is also on google classroom, updated daily. This is pointed out and modeled daily for the first week.

All work is submitted to baskets, labeled by period. This is pointed out and modeled each time work is to be collected.

I personally hand work back, so I can explain or praise achievement.

Students begin work on warm-up as soon as they enter the room. This is modeled and practiced daily for first week.

I wait until students are quiet and looking at me before giving instructions. I move to the vicinity of students if they are not paying attention.

Students sit with their lab partner and perform labs at lab station that is numbered same as their table.

Students wash hands with soap and water at end of each class period, while I spray tables with disinfectant.

(2) 3 Simple Classroom Rules

Be on time.

Be prepared.

Be respectful.

(3) Classroom Discipline Plan

Proactive steps:
1. Get to know students with questionnaire
2. Target specific students daily with personal conversation/genuine connection; track this
3. Circulate room
4. Clear directions; model work
5. Wait until students are attentive
6. Offer choices
7. Specific praise
8. Positive phone calls home to parents; positive notes to students
9. Use Transfer of Students Information Form and/or ask other teachers about students

If more is needed:

Address

Step 1: Redirect/correct student

Step 2: Close proximity to student

Remedy

Step 3: Talk to student privately; can they correct behavior? How? How can I help? Thank you for your maturity and thank you for trying.

Restore

Step 4: Notice and praise new behavior

If proactive steps and A2R does not work:

Step 5: Teacher detention; call parent

Step 6: Building detention

Step 7: Office referral

(4) Classroom Teacher:

Everyone has a unique journey:
- Student questionnaire to get to know their personal likes/dislikes; study habits; family.
- Scientists' stories/Growth mindset activity.
- Describe the person you want to be.
- What advice would you give a friend?

Everyone has potential:
- Offer choices of assignments/projects.
- Specific praise on work/achievement/attempt/collaboration.
- Every student speaks every day.

(continued)

Figure 5.13. Example of Teacher's Classroom Management Plan (*continued*)

Relationships make a difference:
- Greet each student by name at door.
- Learn names by end of 2nd week.
- Positive phone calls home.
- Positive notes to students
- Attend extracurricular activities.
- Approach with "How can I help?"

(5) Golden Concepts

I need to improve on:
- Build relationships.
- With every "relational bridge" that is harmed, circle back to repair it.
- Have more one-on-one interactions.
- Treat every day as a new day, a new start, a new opportunity.
- Don't take things personally; teenagers (all people) make mistakes.
- Smile, laugh, have fun, enjoy the kids.

Change the Environment

Rather than defaulting to the immediate assumption that a misbehaving student is being nothing but defiant or will only change with good old-fashioned discipline, also consider if you could make changes to the student's classroom environment. Making changes in this area could fix your problem! You might consider if there needs to be a change to the seating chart. You might consider changes to your classroom routines or expectations. Perhaps you need to rethink some of your instructional practices. Do you need to do a better job of breaking up activities, modifying assignments, shortening direct instructions, or making lessons more interesting and exciting? Maybe you could use more nonverbal cues or walk around the classroom more often. Sometimes proximity to a student can deter misbehavior. Possibly you need to create smoother transitions between classroom activities. Sometimes a simple change to the classroom environment can alleviate or fix some or most of your discipline challenges.

Change the Relationship

Often your misbehaving students will cooperate more if you make changes to your relationship with them. Do you need to ask these students more nonacademic questions, such as, "What kind of music do you like?" or "How was your weekend?" You might be able to win with some students simply by giving them more attention or providing them with more positive feedback. Some students love to receive praise in front of others. Some students prefer to be left alone. You might need to make changes to your classroom culture. Maybe you can add some simple traditions to your classroom, like a "Fun Friday" or a daily joke. It might be a good idea to incorporate more games into your lessons—to liven things up a bit. You might need to smile more or be more relaxed.

When I was a teacher, my students liked when I would joke around in class. I can have a different sense of humor and would often say eccentric or overly opinionated statements that were meant to solicit a laugh. It made class fun for me and the students! However, I'm human and teaching is tiring. Often, my energy would fade throughout the day, lessening more and more with each class period. Winter is a difficult season for many people. It's cold and dark outside, and we are prone to getting sick. I also coached, so many days I was tired from long days and weeks of working two jobs: teaching and coaching! I discovered that as my energy faded, I would become less likely to joke around with my classes. Often, I wouldn't realize what was happening, but from time to time, I would realize, "Hey, I'm not giving my best self to all of my classes." I'd have to remind myself, "Adam, you need to make it a priority to joke around with each class, nearly every day! That's part of what makes kids like you and a large reason why they enjoy coming to your class." This was a "relationship" component that I needed to change, or rather focus on.

Change the Person

Sometimes we are afforded the awesome opportunity to really impact a student. It can be an "aha" moment for the student; sometimes it can even be somewhat of a life-impacting moment. When you are fortunate enough to go deep with a student in conversation, take advantage of it. A perfectly timed, almost "destined" one-on-one conversation can be an opportunity to help a student make real change. Much of this book seeks to help educators in this area. If you are lucky enough to have the opportunity to help change the behavior of a misbehaving student, not because they must but because they want to, then you have really made a difference. Often, by winning someone over in one instance, you can in effect win them over for a lifetime—truly!

Expectations are essential for students, boundaries are needed, and discipline is often required, but remember that people are changed most often and with the greatest impact by things like patience, grace, second chances, a listening ear, kindness, stories, hope, and mentorship. The best kind of change is if you are able to genuinely influence the person, helping them to see differently and make real behavioral change. You can't force this, but if the timing is right and you have the proper relationship, then seize the moment if you can!

RESOURCE 8: RESET ROOM

At the high school level, we created a reset room to support the social-emotional learning (SEL) needs of certain students. The idea came from a schoolwide inventory assessment and initiative in which school administration worked with all of the teachers to evaluate current SEL programming at the school. Everyone recognized that we were seeing an increase in students who displayed emotional outbursts at school, both in the classroom and in the hallways. Noticing that this was a growing trend, and realizing that suspensions and expulsions weren't the answer for some of these students, the staff began to think "outside of the box." The staff discussed costly programs, such as an emotional disturbance (ED) unit and various vocational-based concepts. Instead of such options, the school decided to implement a low-cost solution that was more in line with the particular student behaviors we were seeing in the school.

After receiving approval from the district office, the high school implemented a reset room, which we called the Student-Centered Support (SCS) resource. We were able to change some room assignments to free up an entire classroom. Fortunately, we already had a licensed social worker employed in the school district. They were moved to the high school full-time and their caseload at the middle school was filled by a newly hired social worker. It was an ideal classroom because it had a separate office space in the room with a large glass window that provided a clear sight of the larger classroom. The social worker was given the office to work with individual students. The larger area of the classroom was used as a reset area. Additionally, we moved a full-time intervention tutor into the larger area of the room to help with supervision and extra support.

The reset room became a schoolwide resource for certain students to report to when they were feeling overly frustrated, angry, anxious, or ready to blow up emotionally. The reset room was a resting place for students who struggled with controlling their emotional responses, whether triggered by something at school or from home. In their office, the social worker would work with students in their caseload. Additionally, other students could go to the room to "let off steam," vent their emotions, and have the space they needed to calm down. Ideally, after a student cooled down, the goal was for the student to learn some coping skills to reduce, avoid, or better handle future emotions, but at a minimum it kept the students away from the remainder of the student body and staff during intense outbursts. *Many* suspensions were avoided because of this resource! Whereas in the past a student might go ballistic in the halls, creating a major disruption, sometimes requiring a building lockdown or police involvement, now students were able to release their emotions in a safe place with a licensed social worker, shielded from the potential to earn a likely suspension. Often, school principals were called to the room to offer additional support to the social worker.

Students had to be approved to use the reset room. We reserved the resource for students who needed it most, many times based on past behaviors that were uniquely disruptive. When they felt their emotions growing out of control, these students were taught, and then expected, to report immediately to the reset room. In most cases, after 20 minutes, although sometimes an hour, and in some cases even an entire day, the students gained composure and were able to return to their regular classes—their emotions were *reset*! Some students were expected to "check in" between classes or at certain points each day to share their concerns about the day and how they were feeling. We utilized "zones of regulation" practices with these "check-ins."

Some teachers joked behind the scenes, referring to the reset room as a "recess room." That's fine. We would remind teachers that it is better to have the students in the "recess room," unleashing their outbursts there, than in *your* classroom! One teacher said it well in a planning meeting:

Some students come to us on particular days with such trauma from what happened in their homes the previous night. How can we expect these students to want to do Math at the moment their emotions trigger horrible memories and frustrations?

If the student misses one class, but avoids a suspension, receives professional counseling, and then can return for the remainder of their classes, then we've accomplished something great with this resource. Figure 5.14 shows the document we used to promote and explain our reset room, the Student-Centered Support resource.

Figure 5.14. Student-Centered Support (Reset) Resource

SCS

Student-Centered Support

DEFINITION

A resource with specialized staff who can provide support to students in need of social–emotional coping skills and de-escalation techniques.

PURPOSE

Due to social–emotional circumstances and different levels of emotional response, some students find it difficult to function within the academic setting at sudden and emerging moments.

SCS seeks to provide individualized supports, interventions, and counseling for students to self-regulate and de-escalate so they can more successfully meet the academic demands of the school environment.

OBJECTIVE

To return the students to class as soon as possible, enabling them to be better situated to learn.

DATA TRACKING

Various systems and tools will be used to monitor student caseload, visits, and progress toward desired student outcomes.

FOCUS AREAS

PROCESSING
Students who self-report or are referred by administration/school counselor to process through sudden and emerging emotional responses that require coping skills and de-escalation techniques.

CHECK-INS
Students who are on a predetermined plan to check into the room to self-regulate and identify their zone of regulation.

SOCIAL WORK COUNSELING
Students who meet one-on-one with a licensed social worker to discuss personal struggles and concerns.

MTSS / RTI
Students who receive academic supports and interventions to accommodate individualized challenges with class assignments.

GROUPS
Students who are invited to participate in group discussions led by a licensed social worker about specific social–emotional topics. This will mostly occur during Academic Period.

LUNCH
Students who receive permission to eat lunch with SCS staff, providing time to build authentic relationships/connections. This also allows students to avoid unwanted lunch room dynamics.

RESOURCE 9: HARASSMENT AND BULLYING REPORT FORM

As school principals know, "harassment" and "bullying" are different from one another. Many people confuse the two terms as being the same. Also, some people incorrectly define each. Bullying is often thought of as being *mean* toward someone. Harassment is often perceived as *bothering* or *pestering* someone. However, bullying is more than being mean and harassment is different from being a nag. Each term is explained by its own legal definition. Harassment is prohibited on a federal level. Bullying is usually prohibited by individual states. Consequently, both harassment and bullying are prohibited by local school board policies.

Generally speaking, *harassment* deals with discriminatory actions or practices toward a class of people. Protected classes include those defined by race, color, national origin, religion, sex, sexual orientation, age, and disability.

Bullying can entail a wide range of behaviors but is usually defined by behaviors that occur *more than once* from a person in a perceived position of power, aimed at a person of perceived lesser power. Additionally, the bullying must be sufficiently severe so that it harms or hinders the victim's mental or physical safety or it harms or hinders their access to a free and appropriate public education. In a bullying situation, there is a said perpetrator and a said victim.

If a bully is inappropriate toward one person just one time and then treats another person poorly at a different time, then his actions probably aren't defined as bullying. Instead, he might have harassed each individual or he might have simply done something that is neither bullying nor harassment, but is nonetheless grossly inappropriate and in violation of another school policy, such as "use of inappropriate language" or "disruptive conduct." School principals must understand these differences as they decide what policy has been violated.

A situation can be bullying instead of harassment or harassment instead of bullying. Some situations can be *both*. If a student is *continually* making racist comments toward or about another student, then it is likely that both definitions will be applied to the case. Many times, a situation is *neither* bullying or harassment. For example, consider a student who says something awful to another student, but it happens only once and it has nothing to do with the other student's race, gender, or any other federally protected category. The student still might receive school discipline, but it wouldn't be for violation of the school's policy on bullying or harassment.

Unfortunately, some states combine harassment and bullying into the same statute, which creates confusion. As a result, schools adopt language from the state statutes into their school policies. This can create confusion because a student might violate a school's "harassment and bullying" policy, but the student's actions met the definition of bullying, not harassment. In a different scenario, a student might have harassed someone, but since it is being applied under the "harassment and bullying" policy, which for many schools usually deal more with bullying, the principal might forget to follow the district's procedures for allegations of harassment, which are dictated by additional statutes and laws. Many times, the procedures for handling cases of harassment are listed in the school district's board of education policy instead of the individual school's student code of conduct. Schools can alleviate this confusion by having a policy on bullying and a separate policy on harassment.

Teachers must understand their role in identifying, addressing, reporting, and preventing these behaviors. School principals must also be skilled at investigating them, deciding when a situation meets the legal definition of each policy, and properly documenting the entire process. Likewise, school principals need to follow specific steps during a harassment or bullying investigation to ensure that the school has complied with *everything* that is required in the fine print of the school board policy. If you are or have been a school administrator, then you know that these policies are quite extensive. Any misstep can open the school up to a lawsuit. Along with special education situations and issues related to constitutional rights, such as student due process, errors in handling allegations of harassment and bullying can become a major liability for modern-day schools.

Because the definitions of bullying and harassment are quite technical, and since the investigations for both are dictated by a multitude of procedures in a school's policies, I decided many years ago to create a "harassment and bullying" form to use when investigating allegations of either term. The main reason I created it was so that I would have a *guide* to ensure that I asked all of the right questions, which could ensure that I followed all of the procedures in the school's policies. In workshops and training, I had received many examples of "reporting" forms, but each of them was very general. As a result, when using them, I might forget to follow and document certain requirements listed in our school's policies. Instead, my form provided *prompts* so that I would remember to ask certain questions and record particular facts. I've used this form at different school districts. At each, I've sifted through the school district's policies on bullying and harassment to make sure that the questions on my form aligned with the legal requirements.

When I receive a student complaint of bullying or harassment, I record their statements under each section on the document. I complete the form on my computer. The form becomes the documentation for the case. Also, it becomes the form that I use to investigate the allegation. Additionally, I use the form as a checklist, making sure I am following all of the required procedures. Lastly, the form becomes the official report for the investigation. I still have the student complete a written report of what happened, but I use this form after they complete the written report, in order to make sure I am addressing each element required by law as it pertains to either bullying or harassment.

This form helps me conduct a thorough and well-documented investigation. The student's answers to the questions help me in deciding if the facts constitute bullying, harassment, both, or something else. Also, the answers help me to better understand the facts, allowing me to create a corrective and supportive plan for the victim.

For example, the first question can be a terrific indicator. Just the other day, a parent called my office and told me that her daughter was being bullied. I immediately met with her daughter. I asked her the first question: "Are you being harassed or bullied?" She said, "No, I'm not being bullied." I explained to her that her mom had called and said that she was being bullied. The student continued, "Well, I can see how it could be seen that way, but no, I'm not being bullied." After asking this first question, I knew we weren't dealing with bullying. Regardless, I continued to interview the student and complete the form (as I always do). I learned that another student called her a mean name. I also learned that she retaliated. Therefore, I was able to discover that both students had acted inappropriately. I crossed bullying off the list, so to speak, and held each student accountable for their own actions. The students were able to reach a peaceful agreement and the case was solved.

Another scenario could be a student who says they are being bullied, but when asked about the frequency, reports that something happened only once. In a different situation, a student might tell me that they are being harassed, but explains that it is not happening at school and isn't impacting them while at school. With that information, the school wouldn't have jurisdiction to get involved, other than to contact their parent/guardian and provide suggestions on how they can respond or who they might want to contact. Another interview might reveal that the complainant sits at the same lunch table as the person they are filing a report on. This information could lead into a discussion about what kind of friends we choose and ways to avoid certain people.

With bullying and harassment, no school can guarantee that every situation is prevented. However, schools must be proactive as they work to prevent cases, and must certainly be timely in investigating every concern, always working to address, support, and remedy cases of bullying and harassment.

If you work with bullying and harassment investigations, especially at the office level, I highly recommend the form shown in Figure 5.15. At each school where I've worked, this form has become the adopted tool for investigating allegations of bullying and harassment. Before using it, make sure it aligns with your school's policies on bullying and harassment and change any of the sections on the form to fit your preferences and needs. It's also a good idea to get it approved by your school principal or district office. This is without a doubt one of the best resources I have created—I highly recommend it for school administrators.

RESOURCE 10: SAFETY PLAN

In some situations, it is good practice to develop and implement an official safety plan for a student. Often, I will write one as a supportive measure for a student who has been bullied or harassed. Sometimes, I'll even write one for situations that haven't been proven, but are alleged or likely. These plans are a great way to document the school's involvement and effort to intervene, especially as it relates to bullying and harassment. Furthermore, they can help a family feel more at ease moving forward. Figure 5.16 is an example safety plan.

Figure 5.15. Harassment / Bullying Report

Harassment / Bullying Report

NAME: ADMIN. INVESTIGATING: DATE:

Are you being harassed or bullied? Do you feel the reason is because of your race/color, religion, national origin, gender, sexual orientation, or disability?

Who is harassing or bullying you? What is happening?

Is the harassment or bullying happening at school? Where? Witnesses?

Are you friends with this person? Do you sit with them at lunch? Do you have classes together? Do you have any mutual friends?

How often does the harassment or bullying happen: daily, weekly, once, twice, a couple of times?

Is it making it hard for you to come to school or learn?

On a level of 1–10, with 1 being not at all and 10 being completely fearful, how much is this threatening your safety or the safety of others?

On a level of 1–10, with 1 being not at all and 10 being unbearable, how much is this bothering your mental or physical well-being?

Have you told an adult about the harassment or bullying before today? If so, who and when?

How can we help with this situation?

Additional details of the harassment or bullying:

_ _

(continued)

Figure 5.15. Harassment / Bullying Report (*continued*)

<u>DETERMINATION:</u>

Check Below:

	Bullying
	Harassment
	Not HIB, but unacceptable behavior/actions
	Mutual conflict between students
	Inconclusive based on evidence/information

- -

<u>ACTION PLAN:</u>

Check Below:	Actions	Details	Date
	School Discipline		
	Warning of Harassment or Bullying		
	No Contact Order or Note of Understanding *(for perpetrator)*		
	Safety Plan *(for victim)*		
	Provide and Explain Board Policy *(for perpetrator)*		
	Provide and Explain Board Policy *(for victim)*		
	Preventative and/or Remedial Measures		
	Training/Education *(for perpetrator)*		
	Training/Education *(for victim)*		
	Mediation		
	Inform necessary school personnel		
	Contact parent/guardian *(for perpetrator)*		
	Contact parent/guardian *(for victim)*		
	Inform District Harassment Coordinator		
	Student Complaint Form, witness statements, additional pieces of evidence/notes/items from investigation on file with administration.		

Figure 5.16. Safety Plan

Safety Plan

For **(Student Name)**

This document is to serve as a Safety Plan agreed to by the student, parent(s)/guardian(s), and the school.

Duration: **(Date)** through the end of the **(year)** school year. This plan may be extended or revised with the agreement of the student, parent(s)/guardian(s), and the school.

1. During school hours, the student is permitted to leave class at any time and immediately report to the guidance office to see a school counselor. If a school counselor is not available, they may request to see an administrator, the school social worker, or another trusted adult.

2. The appropriate teachers have been made aware that should the student ask to leave class, they should subtly permit the student to leave. The student will return directly to class after the necessary supports.

3. The student has identified **(adult staff names)** as safe adults with whom the student can talk to. If seeking to speak with one of them, the student should report to the guidance office and someone in the office will contact one of them. If available, the student is permitted to go speak with them. If unavailable, the student should speak with a school counselor or administrator.

4. The student is permitted to eat their lunch in an area other than the lunchroom. This area must be agreed upon by the student and administration.

5. If the student has any concerns that they have been retaliated against as a result of their complaints of harassment and/or bullying or they are being harassed and/or bullied, the student is to immediately report those concerns to their school counselor or an administrator.

Student Signature _____   Date _____

Parent Signature _____   Date _____

Counselor's Signature _____   Date _____

Administrator's Signature _____   Date _____

Note sent home: _____ via student _____ via email _____ via mail   Date _____

CHAPTER 6

Scenarios

While earning my first graduate degree, I had a professor who would regularly use small case scenarios to teach us complex lessons about school leadership. He could have spent most of our time in class lecturing or reviewing various leadership models, but instead he tried to put us in the shoes of a real-world school principal. I remember him giving us an email, for example, that was written by a fictitious parent, addressed to us who were principals-in-training. He assigned us to small groups, having us discuss how we would respond to the email. I remember him going around the room, asking each group to share their response. After listening to the group, he would point out all of the mistakes they had made! He would explain why doing this or that would likely backfire, or how you should *never* do this, or why you had better not respond that way until you've first spoken with your superintendent. Then, he'd go to the next student group. The next group would share a carefully constructed response filled with politically correct rhetoric. But he'd tear into their ideas, pointing out all the flaws they had failed to foresee. He would do this with every group!

At first, it was comical. But as we continued these exercises—some with emails, some memos, some situational scenarios—he would reveal the complexity that inherently exists in many decision-making moments. He was teaching us that leadership is an art. He was showing us that different situations require varied approaches. We weren't learning knowledge; we were gaining wisdom. It also helped us understand the value that comes from on-the-job experience. When discussing these scenarios, we were able to practice how an effective school leader might respond. We were able to practice as a group under his tutelage.

Inspired by those case scenarios, I began making up my own relating to classroom management and student discipline. I've used them in workshops and seminars, and I've incorporated them into professional development activities with teachers. I've observed some really good discussions among teachers. They have allowed teachers who are skilled at classroom management and at winning with their students to share with other teachers their wonderful strategies and experienced advice. This activity is nonconfrontational, because the teachers who have found success are merely sharing what *they* would do and what *they* have done—not what *you* should do. In this next section, I will share a few of these scenarios. These are not soft cases. They are seriously challenging, but they represent student behaviors that any teacher or administrator might encounter. Being prepared can allow an educator to deal as calmly as possible with situations that might engender panic or anger. These scenarios offer an opportunity to apply perspectives, strategies, and resources found in previous chapters. The ideal approach is to think individually about a response plan and then share and compare with colleagues.

DISCLAIMER

These scenarios focus on specific behaviors, but to allow readers to fully envision encountering each challenge it is helpful to embody each behavior in a hypothetical student. This provides more clarity and helps the audience to better picture themselves in the situation. This book centers on misbehavior, which isn't foreign to anyone with breath in their lungs—misbehavior is part of being human, and certainly part of being a developing youth. This book focuses on how to deal with student misbehavior in a relational and effective way—a way that *wins* with the student. Please don't think that hypothetical Peter or Whitney or Uma or any other student is always impulsive, explosive, or unpleasant. But students can in fact act in such ways and educators need to know how to respond when such misbehaviors appear in the educational setting.

Here are some scenarios related to classroom management and student discipline for educators to think about and discuss:

SCENARIO 1: IMPULSIVE AND DISTRACTED

A student in your class with average to low-average cognitive ability demonstrates an impulse-control, executive-functioning deficit and frequently interrupts your class. You are skilled at setting clear expectations and have very few problems with students not following directions. However, Peter continues to interrupt you and other students. The difficulty is that Peter seems to have good intentions but doesn't seem to realize, let alone succeed at controlling, his interruptions. How would you go about dealing with this situation so that his interruptions aren't a hindrance to the learning of other students?

How about Isaac? Isaac is an average "C" student. He is constantly fidgeting, tapping on the desk, and walking around the classroom. Getting him on task is an enormous challenge. You have corrected him several times, which works for about 15 minutes. It is now a month into the school year and you are no further along with Isaac. What are your next steps?

SCENARIO 2: EXPLOSIVE AND DEFENSIVE

There is a student in your class who can be very explosive. Her name is Whitney. She tends to be rude and is easily "set off." She often talks out of turn and has a tendency to say inappropriate things. When you confront Whitney's behavior, it seems to only make things worse. In fact, you are beginning to dread going to work because this student makes you feel as though you have to "walk on eggshells." If you engage with this student, a battle will likely ensue. You fear a battle will result in her being removed from class, which you want to avoid. What approach do you take with this student?

How would you handle Edward? You're a school administrator. You have a student in your office to discuss a discipline situation. The student's name is Edward. As you begin the conversation, Edward becomes defensive and angry. He senses that he is going to get in a lot of trouble for what he did early in the school day. Edward begins raising his voice. He's cussing, his face is turning red, and he's clenching his fists. He has become very agitated. He hasn't threatened you and you feel safe, but your survival responses are starting to kick in. What should you do?

SCENARIO 3: DISRESPECTFUL AND DEFIANT

Summer Break has come to an end, and as the first day of school approaches you are looking through the names of students who have been assigned to your class. Suddenly, you feel a sense of anxiety and disbelief when your eyes come across the ninth student on your roster. You find out that you have the most disrespectful and defiant student assigned to your class—for the entire year! His name is Derrick. Faithful to his reputation, on the first couple of days of school he is disruptive and rude. When he's not rude, he puts his head down on his desk to sleep. How would you handle this situation?

SCENARIO 4: HARD TO REACH AND RESENTFUL

Hannah has a difficult homelife. It seems like she wants someone to care about her, but she is constantly putting her guard up. You have never seen her smile or appear happy. Actually, she always seems mad and depressed. She shows very little interest in school. She doesn't seem to like you, nor anyone for that matter, and she has little respect for rules and authority. Despite all of this, you have a genuine interest in her and deep down want to see her succeed. You have very clear classroom rules of what students can and can't do in your class. One of those rules deals with the use of cell phones. However, Hannah seems to care very little about your rules, especially as it relates to not using her cell phone. You are struggling with the fact that you want to cut her some slack and ignore her phone behavior, but you don't want her violation of the rules to be seen by the other students. Also, you struggle with the mere fact that she is knowingly breaking a rule that you have made very clear. What are your options?

How will you handle Rachel? In this scenario you can be either a teacher or a principal. Three days ago you had to discipline a student. It resulted in a suspension from school. This student, Rachel, returns to school today. She is still mad at you for suspending her. What should you do? Should you say nothing and act like nothing happened? Should you talk with her? What would you say? How would you approach an interaction with her?

SCENARIO 5: UNPLEASANT, DEFIANT, AND RUDE

Uma has a temper. Every little situation seems to result in an episode of anger. She's rarely friendly, often has a scowl on her face, and she's quick to use vulgarity to make herself heard. She'll talk back to anyone—it doesn't matter if you're a teacher, principal, or even a police officer! Strangely, she seems to get along just fine with her peers. You wonder if she has an issue with authority rather than an all-around lack of interpersonal skills. She openly defies minor school rules. She'll often walk in 30 seconds late to class. During class, she'll listen to music through her headphones even though you expect everyone else to have all personal technology turned off and out of sight. If you say something to her or ask her to be on time to class or put away her music, she'll respond, "Nope." How do you go about dealing with Uma?

Welcome, Reagan! You are having a difficult time with Reagan. She has said several times in class that your rules are stupid. At first, you simply ignored her comment, but now she is beginning to disrupt the learning environment by making this comment. Again, in the middle of class she says loudly, "Your classroom rules are stupid!" How should you handle this?

SCENARIO 6: BEHAVIOR AND SPECTRUM COMBINATION

Benny has an Individualized Education Program (IEP). Your school operates under the belief that although every student is equal, different students require different accommodations and approaches. Your school also emphasizes the practice that general education teachers are not going to dump every IEP concern on the special education teachers. Benny is your student. When he's in your class, you don't have a classroom aide or an intervention specialist in your classroom. Benny has a behavioral goal in his IEP. He is on the Autism spectrum—he is very intelligent, but is easily frustrated by some things that are often trivial to typical students. Benny comes into your classroom and appears agitated. You are not sure what is bothering him, but you notice the tension in his body language. He is murmuring things under his breath, but you can't make sense of his words. Once he gets to his seat, he loudly slams his fist down on the desk. "That must have hurt," you think to yourself. He doesn't appear hurt, but clearly something is going on. You walk over to him and as he sees you approaching he yells, "Get away from me!" You step backwards and remind him to calm down. He yells, "Leave me alone," while standing next to his seat. You encourage him to go into the hallway, but in response he loudly declares, "F-you" (saying the full word)! Good luck with this situation. What do you do now? By the way, all of the other students have arrived in class and are watching.

SCENARIO 7: PUBLICLY DEFIANT

You're a school administrator. You notice a verbal conflict between two students in the hallway. You walk over to defuse the situation. Paul becomes belligerent with you. You tell him that he needs to calm down and can't speak that way. He cusses at you. By this point, he is no longer concerned with the other student. Instead, he is now directing his frustration toward you. Because you are near a large common area in the school, there are more than 50 students walking through the hallways at this moment. Everyone looks over to see what's going on. After Paul cusses at you, you tell him that you need to see him in your office. He tells you to F-off and walks away, clearly defying you in front of all of the other students. You hear kids saying in the background things like, "Oooh" and "Uh oh," while other students snicker. Do you follow him? Do you say something to him? What should you do? By this point, he's halfway down the hallway continuing to walk away.

SCENARIO 8: THE "COUP D'ÉTAT" CLASS

You are 5 weeks into the school year. You are having a hard time with your class. It's been this way since the start of the year. You aren't struggling with just one or a few students. You are having discipline issues with six different students, each to varying degrees. Nearly half of the class is participating in the daily chaos and regular disruptions. Sometimes you wonder if they are planning a coup d'état! "What in the world is going on?" you wonder. You ask yourself, "Have I done something wrong or is this just bad luck?" You consider, "Did the principal purposefully give me the most difficult class roster?" What path should you take?

SCENARIO 9: RAGING

In this scenario you can be either a teacher or a principal. Ronald has become explosive. He's pushed over a chair, he's yelling, and he's reached a point of rage. You are worried he might punch something or even someone. You are not comfortable getting too close to him because you don't know what he might do. If this is in your classroom with other students around, what should you do? You will probably call for an administrator, but how will you do that and what will you do before the administrator gets to your room? If you are a principal and this happens in your office where no other student is around, what would you do?

SCENARIO 10: BAD REPUTATION AND SLY

Brianna is a new student. She just enrolled and Winter Break is soon approaching. She doesn't know anyone at the school. The first day she is quiet in class. During her first day, after you have had her in class, you talk to the school counselor and you learn that Brianna had a host of discipline issues at her old school. Another teacher tells you that they "heard" that Brianna was expelled from a school 2 or 3 years ago. What steps might you take to prepare for tomorrow's class with Brianna? How might you interact with her the next day?

Please meet "Sly" Sebastian. You've been warned by his previous teachers that Sebastian has a reputation for lying. They have told you that it can be a challenge dealing with him because he can be quite insubordinate, but he is very intelligent and knows how to "work the system." One teacher tells you that they got into a big mess with him and the principal last year because he lied about what happened in class one day and they (the teacher) nearly got in trouble based on Sebastian's accusations. As a result, Sebastian was able to "take over" the classroom from that point forward because the teacher was too afraid to challenge his misbehavior out of fear that he would twist things if they tried to discipline him. His classroom insubordination didn't warrant a suspension or raise any major red flags, but it was just inappropriate, disruptive, and constant. The teacher tells you that it was one of the worst years in their entire career. What steps should you take so that their experience doesn't become your experience?

Conclusion

This book isn't meant to further academic research or unveil a new finding. I wrote this book to help teachers! I wrote it to help other school administrators! This book converts presentations I've given throughout the years into more accessible form. It shares a multitude of "tricks of the trade"—lessons I've learned through nearly 2 decades of work with students. If we can't *win* with misbehaving students, then our jobs will become increasingly difficult and our personal burnout will quicken upon us. In the process, we will miss endless opportunities to positively impact students who desperately need our help.

Classroom management is not about having the right *rules*; it's about having the right *relationships*. For many students you might be the only steady force in their life. Their home lives are chaotic, their emotions are confusing, their situations are frustrating, and on top of all this, they lack wisdom and experience. "These children have no life options for achieving decent lives other than by experiencing success at school" (Haberman, 1995, p. 1). Discipline—that is, holding students accountable in a relational way—can be the best opportunity to show them a consistent, calm "I'm here to help and guide you" example. Through continual use and refinement, relational discipline that is non-punitive is an art that can become a science. It can become so habitual that your ability to *win* with students can become almost automatic. Effective discipline practices that are relationally based and skillfully applied can make a huge difference, changing the behaviors of many misbehaving students. In closing, I wish the absolute best for every educator and student! May you *win* with every student, especially misbehaving students!

References

Boykin, A. W., & Noguera, P. (2011). *Creating the opportunity to learn: Moving from research to practice to close the achievement gap.* ASCD.

Camera, L. (2020, October 13). School suspension data shows glaring disparities in discipline by race. *U.S. News.* https://www.usnews.com/news/education-news/articles/2020-10-13/school-suspension-data-shows-glaring-disparities-in-discipline-by-race

Carnegie, D. (1936). *How to win friends and influence people.* Pocket Books.

Dewey, J. (1938). *Experience and education.* The Macmillan Company.

Flannery, M. E. (2015, January 5). The school-to-prison pipeline: Time to shut it down. https://www.nea.org/advocating-for-change/new-from-nea/school-prison-pipeline-time-shut-it-down

Gardner, A. (2012). *Change your words, change your world.* Hay House.

Haberman, M. (1995). *Star teachers of children in poverty.* Kappa Delta Pi.

Irvine, J. J. (1990). *Black students and school failure: Policies, practices, and prescriptions.* Greenwood Press.

Lehman, J. (n.d.). *Disrespectful kids and teens: 5 rules to help you handle their behavior.* Empowering Parents. https://www.empoweringparents.com/article/disrespectful-kids-and-teens-5-rules-to-help-you-handle-their-behavior/

Macmillan. d.y. Blow smoke. In *Macmillan Dictionary.* Retrieved from ttps://www.macmillandictionary.com/us/dictionary/american/blow-smoke

Payne, R. (2018). *Emotional poverty in all demographics: How to reduce anger, anxiety, and violence in the classroom.* aha! Process.

Pranis, K. (2005). *The little book of circle processes: A new/old approach to peacemaking.* Good Books.

Rogers, F. (2019). *A beautiful day in the neighborhood: Neighborly words of wisdom from Mister Rogers.* Penguin Books.

Searle, M. (2013). *Causes and cures in the classroom: Getting to the root of academic and behavior problems.* ASCD.

Senge, P. M., Cambron-McCabe, N. H., Lucas, T., Smith, B., Dutton, J., & Kleiner, A. (2012). *Schools that learn: A fifth discipline fieldbook for educators, parents, and everyone who cares about education.* Crown Business.

Ware, F. (2006). Warm demander pedagogy: Culturally responsive teaching that supports a culture of achievement for African American students. *Urban Education, 41*(4), 427–456. https://doi.org/10.1177/0042085906289710

Wong, H. K., & Wong, R. T. (2001). *The first days of school: How to be an effective teacher.* Harry K. Wong Publications.

Zehr, H. (2005). *The little book of restorative justice.* Good Books.

Index

About the Author

Adam H. Frank, PhD, is principal at Palmer Ridge High School in Monument, Colorado. He's been an assistant principal, athletic director, dean of students, varsity head coach, and taught social studies (grades 6–12). He's worked in two states and has experience at high schools in five school districts. The districts include urban, suburban, and rural settings and represent a wide range of cultural, racial, and socio economic diversity.

He earned his PhD in educational leadership with a focus in change theory and authentic, transformational leadership from Miami University (OH). He holds three educational licenses in Colorado.

Dr. Frank is an authentic leader who believes in realistic and humanistic communication. His approach to leadership and organizational management is progressive, yet practical. A common framework he promotes is "structured flexibility." He has experience leading change initiatives while garnering widespread collaboration with high trust and morale. As a life-long educator, he is passionately student-centered. He values the unique impact teachers can have on students, and he believes in public education.

Dr. Frank provides consulting, speaking, and professional development services in addition to authorship. He is an active practitioner who loves to see educators grow and students flourish. He specializes in school discipline, legal practices, student-centered engagement, leadership development, and change theory. You can contact him on Twitter at @DrAdamFrank or through email at adamfrank1212@gmail.com, or you can visit his website: https://www.dradamfrank.com.